# The Boundless Resource

# The Boundless Resource
## A PROSPECTUS FOR AN EDUCATION-WORK POLICY

WILLARD WIRTZ
and the National Manpower Institute

THE NEW REPUBLIC BOOK COMPANY, INC. Washington, D.C.

Published in the United States of America in 1975
by The New Republic Book Company, Inc.
1826 Jefferson Place, N.W., Washington, D.C. 20036

© 1975 by The National Manpower Institute

**Library of Congress Cataloging in Publication Data**

Wirtz, William Willard, 1912-
    The boundless resource.

    Includes bibliographical references and index.
    1. Industry and education—United States.    2. Adult
education—United States.    I. National Manpower Insti-
tute.    II. Title.
LC1085.W57        370.11'3        75-30556
ISBN 0-915220-07-5
ISBN 0-915220-10-5 pbk.

Printed in the United States of America

# Preface

We made the writing of this Prospectus a testing of its central doctrine: that the key to bringing education and work closer together is not so much in any particular programs as in developing truly *collaborative processes* among those in charge of these functions, including the "public."

Seven times during the course of the shaping of the Prospectus, a Council of some twenty-four members met—for two days or sometimes three—to discuss various aspects of the subject and to go over drafts that had been prepared. Ten Council members came from industry, nine had essentially educational experience, and five of us were sufficiently unclassifiable to be considered representatives of "the public." There had been an earlier meeting at which a smaller group, similarly differentiated, had blocked out a tentative approach in broad terms.

There was sharp and broad disagreement within the Council at first about almost everything. But the realized consensus broadened at each meeting. It became, significantly, larger as we moved from the discussion of general principles to a consideration of specific proposals, and the realization that this was happening encouraged the effort.

There is no reason to detail this story beyond making it clear that what is here in its final form, and must stand on its own feet, is the product of a genuine group effort. The Prospectus is a fair example of what the process it recommends can be expected to produce.

The understanding among the Council members became so

complete that it was not necessary to work out any formal agreement about "endorsement" of the Prospectus. It would be true of all of us that we would be inclined to express and handle differently *particular points* made in the Prospectus, but that we would at the same time consider what is here a sufficiently reliable and significant consensus among people with disparate interests and responsibilities that it is to be preferred above any further pressing of personal predilections.

In response to the spirit that came to preside over these Council deliberations, the members are listed without their titular distinctions and simply in an order the alphabet provides (but with a difference commended to the chairman by his having lived always at the end of it):

> Grant Venn, Georgia State University
> Lewis Solmon, Higher Education Research Institute
> Patrick J. Scollard, Equitable Life Assurance Society
> James O'Toole, Center for Futures Research, University of Southern California
> Marilyn Levy, Rockefeller Brothers Fund
> R.B. Lapham, Burroughs Corporation
> Clement P. Kerley, Pitney Bowes Corporation
> William C. Kelly, National Academy of Sciences
> Beverly B. Johnson, Atlanta Public Schools
> Jack Golodner, Council of AFL-CIO Unions for Professional Employees
> Lawrence Givens, Chrysler Corporation
> John N. Gentry, National Manpower Institute
> Russell S. Fox, Textron, Inc.
> Francis D. Fisher, Harvard University
> Martin W. Essex, Ohio Department of Education
> E. Alden Dunham, Carnegie Corporation of New York
> John Chadwell, Owens-Illinois, Inc.
> Bruce Carswell, GTE Sylvania, Incorporated
> George H. Brown, The Conference Board
> Charles R. Bowen, International Business Machines Corporation
> Marvin H. Berkeley, North Texas State University
> Paul E. Barton, National Manpower Institute
> Wilton Anderson, Washington Technical Institute

This emphasis on the unusual role of the Council in this enterprise might seem to diminish the critical part played here by the Institute staff. It was really the relationship between these two groups, particularly the mutuality of their respect, that was distinctive. The

Council worked with raw materials the staff developed and did not itself attempt to write a book. When, however, the advice was—at one point—to go back to the drawing board and start over, this was done.

Four of us—including John N. Gentry, Dennis Gallagher, and most particularly Paul E. Barton—shared continuing responsibility for shaping both the process and the product that developed from it. We had the extraordinarily competent and conscientious help of our day-to-day associates who, being the kind of people they are, would dislike a labored recital of the very different parts they played: Ted Youn, Leo R. Werts, Terry Unruh, Nancy Swann, Mary McIntosh, Arlene Huff, Harold Goldstein, Julia French, and—again in particular—Stephanie Cole and Catherine Bell.

We knew that the purpose we had set ourselves could be only partially achieved: to synthesize the available experience and commentary about education and work, to add something of the results of our own thinking, to reach with the Council a set of specific recommendations consistent with both principle and pragmatism, and to put all of this in reasonably readable and, in any event, compact form.

The hardest part of it was what had to be left out. Most points made in the Prospectus have been, in themselves, more fully developed someplace else; there are short paragraphs or even single sentences here that barely suggest broad areas warranting thorough examination. It seemed increasingly as the project proceeded, though, that what is most critically important at this stage in this particular attempt at social engineering is putting the *whole* of the education-work prospect sufficiently together that we can get beyond spending so much time and energy on little pieces of it.

The other major demand was that there had to be an adjustment in midcourse to the impact on this inquiry of a virtual doubling of the national unemployment rate. Some answers to particular education-work problems that had seemed easy in the context of the "full employment" euphoria that attended the initiation of the project emerged as simply irrelevant under the testing of an increase in the unemployment rate to 9 percent. While the discipline imposed by the recession extended the project some, it unquestionably strengthened the effort.

It perhaps strains a preface's proprieties to remark, even this briefly, on the personal pleasures and satisfactions that come from and to a small group of people working together on something like this—in the hope that things will conceivably be a little better for the effort.

## Preface

There was also invaluable assistance in this project—of varying nature—from George A. Spater, G. William Miller, James Hodgson, Robben W. Fleming, and William M. Dietel at the genesis; from John I. Goodlad, John T. Dunlop, and Howard R. Bowen at various points along the way; and from Joan Tapper and particularly Calvin Kytle as we reached the Book of Job.

This has been, as these things go, an expensive venture. The Rockefeller Brothers Fund and the Carnegie Corporation of New York provided most of the funding, and there was also a grant from Harvard University. The rest of it came from the National Manpower Institute's corporate sponsors, particularly through the offices of Leslie Warner and George W. Griffin, Jr., of General Telephone and Electronics Corporation.

Finally of those whose contribution to anything of this kind always takes forms rebuking attempted description. In one way or another, wives and husbands of those listed here played large roles in the development of this document, so that while a personal dedication would violate its nature, Jane Quisenberry Wirtz is appropriately recognized as representative of this group of the largest of all our creditors.

*Washington, D.C.*
*August 1975*

WILLARD WIRTZ

# Foreword *
## BY JOHN T. DUNLOP

This is a significant volume because of the auspices under which it has been produced, the process by which it was written, and its perceptive analysis and recommendations for private and public policy.

The work is the product of the National Manpower Institute, which was established in 1970 by a group of business leaders, academic administrators, and others seeking to bridge the gap between education and work. This endeavor began with the conviction that the conventional separation of school and work is detrimental to youth and adults alike and that bringing together concerned individuals from the institutions that govern both worlds would yield insightful analysis and new practical programs. The process from which this work resulted included a discussion of ideas periodically for several years in a dedicated group drawn from business, education, labor, and government. The analyses in the first two parts of the book are followed by a series of specific program proposals, and a final chapter provides a practical agenda for private and public policy, both for the immediate future and the long term.

In the American environment our economic strength historically has been based upon a partnership of dynamic business investment and technology, unparalleled opportunities for education and training, and a highly motivated work force seeking to improve its

---

*This volume was complete, save for editing, in mid-March 1975 when I entered the government on a full-time basis and resigned, after five years of association, as Chairman of the Board of Trustees of the National Manpower Institute.

capacities and advance its living standards in gainful employment. Each period reassesses the arrangements of this partnership to extend opportunities to neglected groups of our citizens and to build new institutions and review others to make the partnership more effective, as was done by the land grant colleges, vocational education, the junior colleges, and the manpower programs of the past decade.

In recent years there has been a growing view that public education and training poorly prepare youth for work. Unemployment among young workers sixteen to nineteen years of age, which runs three times the average of all workers, makes us wonder whether the fault lies with educational institutions or in the labor market. More than a third of vocational school graduates are still trained for agriculture or home economics, and there is appropriate concern over the way in which employment prospects in the real world are reflected in vocational education and counseling. Manpower and vocational education programs are too often perceived as "holding operations" for the disadvantaged. Where formal public vocational preparation has failed to meet the needs and aspirations of both workers and employers, a considerable private "shadow system" has emerged as a substitute, better relating education and work. The major components are programs of on-the-job training, formal programs of education organized by employers, "for-profit" vocational schools and vocational training in the military services, and apprenticeship.

At the same time that there is dissatisfaction with the nexus between education and work for initial job entry for youth, there is new interest in educational opportunities for those already with jobs who seek more interesting or rewarding work and lives. This volume reminds us that there are 51 million adults in this country who have had less than twelve years of formal schooling. In 1900 no more than 4 percent of the age group were in higher education; in 1940 the figure was 16 percent, and today it is approximately half. There is a large backlog of educational interests in our mature citizens, especially among women and minorities, that requires new organizational arrangements between work and education.

As these concerns for youth and adults have grown in recent years, so has our appreciation of the complexities of the interactions of school and work. Almost three-fourths of teenage employment has been concentrated in four occupational areas—clerical work, semi-skilled operations, service, work and laborers' activities—low-paying, unskilled operations. An aging process seems to develop, and these same youth in three or four years time move up to higher-skilled and better-paid occupations as they develop work experience. This volume is directed toward enhancing our understanding of these patterns of movement and improving our judgments as to appropriate private and public policies to facilitate the transition from educational institutions to more productive work.

We have also learned that the traditional pattern of school first and then employment is rapidly changing. Youth are increasingly both in school and at work part time. There is the suggestion now that "the time is coming when teenage employment and unemployment will for the most part be identified with the schooling period of life, rather than reflecting the movement from school and entry into adulthood, as in times past."

A number of developments in recent years help to provide the ingredients of a new relationship between work and education: the new interest in career education in our schools, the growth of cooperative education and the increasing respectability of periods of work away from school during the higher education years, improved occupational information and longitudinal studies of careers over long periods of time, and local and state manpower planning represented by the Comprehensive Employment and Training Act. It should now be possible to put together from these elements a new and more viable partnership for work and education.

President Ford, a few weeks in office, on August 30, 1974, called attention to the basic importance of the nexus of work and education in his speech at the summer commencement of Ohio State University. "I will do everything in my power to bring education and employers together in a new climate of credibility—an atmosphere in which universities turn out scholars and employers turn them on. . . . I have asked the Secretaries of Commerce, Labor and HEW to report to me new ways to bring the world of work and the institutions of education closer together."

The time has indeed come in local communities and states to bring together manpower and education planning, to provide career advising within context of the realities of the longer-term labor market, and to relate systematically business managements, labor organizations, and our formal educational institutions with the arrangements for private training and skill acquisition. This Prospectus provides detailed and practical suggestions to private and public policy-makers alike.

Mr. Wirtz brought to the National Manpower Institute a lifetime of involvement and concern with education; he was the moving spirit in the genesis of an active governmental manpower policy in the 1960s as Secretary of Labor, and his familiarity with and respect for labor and management institutions derived from extensive experience in the collective bargaining process. This rich experience has provided the leadership to shape the substantive analysis and recommendations. The volume has the further virtue that it is a delight to read, reflecting a sensitive style and rare creative perspective.

*Washington, D. C.*                                                JOHN T. DUNLOP
*August 1975*

# Contents

# The Boundless Resource

# Introduction:
## A NEW IMPERATIVE,
## A NEW PROSPECT

A good deal of the American achievement traces in one way or another to the development of Education and Work as coordinate forces. They have, however, been distinctively separate developments controlled by independent institutional sovereignties—with the consequence that in most people's lives learning and earning pass as totally isolated chapters.

This traditional separatism has come under increasing challenge. Young people encounter worsening difficulty moving from school to jobs, a situation generally attributed to the fact that the two functions have gotten out of kilter. Among adults—women completing maternity service, mature blacks freed by law of their collective bondage but still imprisoned by individual circumstance, middle-aged men and women wanting to change their career courses, older people looking for new opportunity as well as for security—there is a new chafing against the constraints inherent in the tradition that marks education For Children Only. The vague public awareness of a decade ago of the human costs in compartmentalizing education and work is today developing into a consensus that the two systems be brought together.

So far, the efforts to do this have been concentrated mostly at the place where the need has been felt the most—at the point of passage between youth and adulthood. For some years more and more young people have been preparing themselves for futures that have No Help Wanted signs up when they get there. Other jobs, meanwhile, have gone begging. More than a third of all reported unemployment in the

1

Introduction

country has been among sixteen-to-twenty-one-year-olds. No comparable situation exists in any other developed nation in the world.

To reverse this trend, various ideas and programs—all parts of a common attempt "to build bridges between the two worlds of education and work"—have been introduced. School curricula have been expanded to include more work study and cooperative education programs and to reflect a more broadly conceived concern for career education. We have built more vocational high schools, and added a brand-new tier of technically oriented two-year colleges to the education structure. An affirmative manpower training program has brought the Jobs Corps, the Neighborhood Youth Corps, and JOBS (Job Opportunities in the Business Sector), all centered on problems at the school-job passage.

The measurable effect, of most such efforts has been so limited as to rebuke the rhetoric they draw on. "Experiential learning" is still a phrase looking for its specific content. More and more the federal manpower training programs have become merely systems for public employment or income transfer. By recent report 4 million teachers will be trained during the 1970s for what will be only 2 million grade and high school openings. Satisfaction that more young people are now going on to college is sobered by a projection that in percentage terms the number of college graduates is increasing faster than the number of jobs traditionally requiring a college education. The youth unemployment rate has moved up to an unprecedented 20 percent—to more than 40 percent among those who are both young and black.

Clearly, the decay at the bridges between education and work has proceeded faster than have the bridge builders.

Now, suddenly, the significance of these floundering efforts has taken on a whole new dimension. Startled at having overslept, we have awakened to the realization that the governing idea of growth—the idea that motivated and energized our development as a nation—will have to be redefined. The closing of valves on fossil fuel lines in another part of the world serves grim notice that the natural resources that we have mistakenly relied on as the raw materials for limitless growth are in dwindling supply. There is no mistaking the warnings. It isn't just the youth unemployment rate that has shot up; unemployment in the country as a whole is higher than in three and a half decades.

What this means, almost ironically, is that what we have been attacking as a problem of moving youth from schoolrooms to jobs is

2

in reality the much broader predicament for the whole lot of us.

The depletion of natural resources leaves us only two choices. One, plainly, is to shrink—which is against our nature and probably contrary to the laws of institutional or system survival. The other, no less plain, is to rebuild our ideas and plans around the fuller development of those other resources which are called "human" and which are in limitless supply.

Just what this alternative involves is by no means clear. We haven't thought about it nearly enough. Reliance on a fuller use of the human resource is, however, precisely what the interrelating of education and work is all about. What some of us have been working on at the gap between schoolroom and job now becomes the nation's assignment. Any necessary discipline is in a recognition of the alternatives. The new American imperative commends the new American prospect: of growth unlimited, based on the fuller development of what is inside people as individuals, through a new coordination of the classically equal but separate forces of education and work.

Consideration of this prospect requires clear understanding on two points:

An education-work policy is not one that misconceives of education as having for its purpose the preparation of people for work. Rather, it *includes* this purpose as part of education's function of preparing people for life, of which work is one part; it takes full account of learning as a human value in itself. Nor is education conceived of here solely in its institutionalized sense.

"Work" is similarly used—not in any narrow vocational sense, although, again, it *includes* vocational values as an important aspect of work. It refers not to a given but to a changing function, and it refers to labor not only as a unit of production but as a human value.

The other point to make clear is that the prospect suggested here is not fully perceived in terms of what it takes to make a system or society function. Such perception is essential, but as a means not an end. To identify the human resource as an essential ingredient of systemic growth is in no way to confuse the priorities of individual and institutional interests. The superior claim on reason of this different growth concept is that to develop people's capacities more fully inevitably increases their prospects for *a higher, better, and more satisfying life experience.*

A decent respect for the opinions of history, however, requires that full reliance be placed neither on the logic of a new economics of growth based on development of the human resource, nor on a new

3

ethic based on the potential for a richer life experience. The sternest law of social change is that it is effective only as it starts from things as they are, depending no more than for spiritual counsel on what they ought to be.

The place to start toward a more productive interrelating of education and work remains at that critical passage through which young people move from school to jobs. This is not where the real roots of the difficulty lie. But it is here that the gap between the two worlds is now most clearly perceived. It is here that the problems surface in a way they can be dealt with. And it is here that processes can be most readily designed that, while meeting immediate needs, are of a nature to permit later application to the deeper causes and longer-range prospects. It is at the youth passage that we have had the most institutional experience, and it will be out of this experience, rather than from any broader logic, that more comprehensive programs will take shape.

So it is important, first, to determine how far the efforts to date have carried, and what they suggest of how they can be most effectively improved on. A review of them suggests three general conclusions:

First: The *program* elements in an effective education-work policy directed at these problems at the school-to-employment gap have now been pretty well marked out.

But second: The *process* elements that are manifestly essential to the effective administration of these new programs have *not* been significantly developed. While the programs bridge the "two worlds," the handling of them so far has been left largely in one of these worlds, education, alone.

And third: There has been very little development of those mundane but critical *measurement and evaluation* procedures that are essential both to identify what needs to be done and to determine the effectiveness of whatever efforts are made at doing it.

So far as the program aspects of this phase of an education-work policy are concerned, attention has centered particularly on the need for a larger element of experiential learning in the educational curriculum, particularly in the high school and early postsecondary grades, during what is roughly the sixteen-to-nineteen-year age period. It's now generally considered a good thing for every boy and girl to have some form of meaningful work experience. Career education, introduced in 1971 by then U.S. Commissioner of Education, Sidney Marland, assumes the broader view that these experiences should provide exposure throughout the school years to what the world of work is all about. The past few years have seen a rapid expansion of technical high schools and two-year colleges, perhaps the most significant reflection to date of the relatively new public commitment to provide an opportunity—as part of the general educational program—for those young people who do not expect to complete college to prepare themselves for particular occupations.

Another now clearly identified program requirement is for the development of fuller information about future manpower needs, of a sort to describe the occupational or career prospects of young people presently in training, with the accompanying necessity of an adequate system for getting this information into the hands of both students and those who are shaping the educational offerings. There hasn't been much change, though, with respect to either part of this picture. The projections of *future* needs remain seriously inadequate, especially with respect to local (as compared with nationwide) employment prospects. The critical function of vocational guidance and counseling, particularly at the high school level, is recognized as probably more inadequately supplied than any other; but very little has been done about it.

Yet whatever may be the remaining program deficiencies, the most serious of them trace to the continuing reliance, so far, on what are virtually unilateral efforts within the educational system alone to do what is now recognized as a function clearly involving *both* education and work. Employers are called on to provide opportunities for work-study and cooperative education, largely in the name of "corporate social consciousness," but in no sense do they become full partners in the joint enterprise. The high schools have apparently accepted a responsibility for vocational guidance and counseling that, acting alone, they are simply not equipped to provide. Yet, virtually every community in the country has an untapped reservoir of personnel and information that could make both vocational guidance and job placement effective for young people, at least within the limits of their training and the supply of work opportunities. What is lacking is the requisite collaborative process.

The clearest lesson from the initiatives so far taken is that such bridges can't be built only from one side. There won't be a really meaningful education-work policy until there are developed *collaborative processes* for both the devising and the administering of these "two-world" programs. Beyond this, there is the strong likelihood that to be truly effective these new processes will have to be developed along lines that include a reactivation of the *public* interest in this whole area. For this, some new forms of direct participation by the broader community membership will have to be devised.

There must be new programs, then, and equally new processes, and sooner or later—with only limited prospects until this is attended to—new *measurements* as well. The architects of social change seem to ignore that their efforts won't bring much change, except as some emergency develops, unless they can prove their case. No one seems to realize how much this depends on some form of statistical measurement of whatever is done, and how much the present measurements of education and work are tied in with, and tend to support, the present way of doing things. The education and employment measurements in use today are essentially head counts; they show littie about the value or the quality of whatever is in these heads or what the heads might be doing. Despite all the efforts of the past decade to tie the education and work functions more closely together—to improve youths' prospects and competencies—we have only the flimsiest records of what these efforts have accomplished. Yet such measurements could be made comparatively easily, and the case would then, assuming it is right, be infinitely stronger.

So far as the decade's bridge-building is concerned, then, whereas the pieces are in place the building has only started.

Now there is a new critical economic circumstance, with an initial impact that is plainly adverse. Massive layoffs in American industry are met by a last-in-first-out policy that puts the particular brunt of it on the youngest members of the work force. Work-study, cooperative education, and special youth job opportunity programs run into the sobering fact that employers simply cannot provide experiential learning slots for high school and college students when employees with seniority are on the unemployment rolls. Better vocational guidance and counseling? For what? New bridges? To where?

Today there is the very real prospect that part of the readjustment to a new meaning of growth will involve a particular and basic change in the direction of individuals' energies and activities during this traditional transition between youth and adulthood.

Will it become advisable that still more young people spend more time in formal education? With perhaps more of it going to *both* general and vocational preparation? Perhaps.

Will these new developments commend further consideration of a national service opportunity—even requirement—in place of the military service so many young Americans have faced in the past? But possibly in a different form—developed locally instead of nationally—perhaps as community internships or apprenticeships?

What will be the different form of vocational or career education if it develops that a changing meaning of growth includes a significantly larger element of "service" than the conventional meaning did? And if that different meaning gives a larger importance to things people do outside the "labor market?"

To look carefully at this bridge-building at the traditional gap between youth and maturity is to realize that the two worlds of education and work will be drawn together significantly only as it is recognized that this offers at least as much promise to the enhancement of adulthood as it does to the improvement of youth. The considerations here are rooted as much in political pragmatism as in philosophical humanism. Vast opportunities exist both to enlarge the human prospect and to increase the value to the economy of the human resource by extending the educational privilege to include adults as well as young people. As a practical political matter, however, the new processes essential to an effective interrelationship of education and work can be achieved only through the organization of a working majority who can identify some self-interest in the process. The acceptance of a meaningful education-work policy depends on identifying and mobilizing a coalition constituency for change.

To love life greatly is to realize no less clearly that for many people it would make as much sense if life were lived the other way around: so that we came shuffling into it at age seventy-five or eighty; went first through those ten or fifteen years nobody has yet figured out the use for; moved after that rough initiation on to forty years or so of reasonably satisfying, if not easy, productiveness; entered then the doors to twelve or eighteen years of exciting learning and discovery; topped this off with a few years of love but little consequence; and had the doctor at the end of it pick us up by the heels and pat us goodbye instead of hello.

Impious fantasy, of course. Not, however, with imagery's license, without its point. For putting life into three time traps—education, then work, then obsolescence—is a human convention that became reality because it first became custom.

A century ago, when universal education was part of a vigorous young nation's boast before the world, there was good reason for making schooling something everybody completed before moving on to whatever was to follow, never to return. There is no reason at all for this now. What was original good sense has become a frustrating and expensive anachronism.

The education that was the subject of principal consideration in the mid-nineteenth century was largely elementary learning, covering only those essentials that obviously have to come at the beginning. It was decided that ten years of it would be about right, which happened to coincide with the physiology of the strengthening of a boy's arm and back muscles and a girl's coming of child-bearing age. The logical place for what education meant then, for most people, was right at the start, and there was no place for any more later.

Today the educational norm is not ten years but fourteen to sixteen, and it covers a good deal more than the basic three Rs. It is by no means clear that what is now being covered can be best absorbed by every human system at one long sitting. It is clearer that it can't be. One of the inevitable incidents of the innovations being made in the school-to-work area will be the abolition of the shibboleth that everybody should "stay in school until you're finished." That idea has already crumbled and cracked to the point that it is now held together mostly by a combination of administrative convenience and false parental pride and concern.

A next order of business is working out the arrangements—by no means simple, yet not all that hard—for permitting and even encouraging those young people for whom it makes sense to build a considered break into their academic sequence; so that they move out of school for a year or two, occasionally even longer, and then move back in. One of the most interesting recent developments, its implications still little recognized, is the tuition-refund practice being followed by more and more large corporate employers. Under this practice, employers reimburse workers for the tuition costs of work-related study.

A more basic change is called for in the nature of the adult experience. To an extent considerably exceeding our realization of it, most of us take work as a given, something that exists and develops as the consequence of forces outside our control. In this sense we think of it differently from the way we think about education. Education we recognize more as within our jurisdiction, and so to be adjusted to work. This concept of work is wrong to begin with, and stands in the way of fully rational education-work policy-making. Because the changing nature of work is insufficiently recognized, the tendency is to develop vocational and even career educational planning around meanings that work may already have lost.

The short of it is that some kind of provision for interspersing the earning and learning of a living, for interweaving employment and self-renewal, is going to have to be recognized as the essential condition for an effective career as worker, citizen, or human being.

These prospects are only barely suggested by what has been thought of so far in terms of adult education. There are, to be sure, impressively large figures, in the tens of millions, for the numbers of adults taking courses of one kind or another that come within this description. A significant amount of this is going on, and here again it will be this already developing experience that offers the basis for future building. But on closer scrutiny it turns out that the very large part of what is covered by these impressively large figures is either (1) training taken to improve people's competence in whatever they are already doing, or (2) some comparatively narrow and superficial exposure to essentially peripheral interests. Both are important. But they don't even touch on the really basic elements in this situation.

Two other sets of relevant figures have the infirmities that all isolated statistics and facts are prey to. They do, nevertheless, come closer to suggesting both the important truth that life has gotten divided into the time traps of youth for education, adulthood for work, old age for nothing and also the dimensions of the prospect for doing something about it.

Consider: There are 51 million adults in this country today who have had less than twelve years of formal education—that span of education available to all Americans, provided they take it when they're young.

Less precisely but more significantly: Seventy-five years ago, at the turn of the century, waking hours for the vast majority of adults were completely dominated by the demands and rigors of making a living and raising a family. Moreover most people, men and women alike, were engaged in substantially the same occupation when they approached the end of the adult experience as they were at its beginning. Today, however: (1) earning a living and raising a family occupy—for men and women alike—*about one third* of an adult's waking hours; (2) most women will have only two instead of five children; and (3) most men will shift from first one to another to a third occupation to earn their livelihoods. In 1900 at least one parent was dead before the youngest child reached the age of twenty-one. Today, most parents can look forward to about two decades of life *after* the last child has grown up and moved away.

Other figures offer a different insight into what is happening here— the extraordinarily rapid rise in the "educational attainment level" of adults. In 1970, 10 million men and women in the American work force (one out of every eight) had completed a college education or more; ten years from now, this number will have increased to 19 million (about one in five). Conversely, where in 1970 there were about 14.5 million with only an eighth-grade education or less, this will have decreased by 1990 to about 5.6 million, one out of twenty. This change is even more rapid among women, including both those in and those outside the work force as it is customarily measured.

These figures suggest, but only suggest, the changes in the nature of work and of the adult life of which work is still an important but no longer the possessively dominant part. That in the light of these changes education should still be provided as a service available almost exclusively to the young is an anachronism and a scandalous waste. We haven't the vaguest notion of the number of people (only that it is exceedingly large) who come—someplace between the ages of twenty-five and fifty—to a point of significant realization that they ought to be on a different career course, not just as a matter of boredom or frustration or some kind of whim, but as a calculated judgment about improving their worth both to themselves and to the whole system. Sometimes this conclusion is the dictate of external circumstance: A machine is doing now what the individual had been doing before. Sometimes it is merely the delayed effort to find out more than was clear the day after graduation (or some less dignified academic exit) what the individual's real capacities—and interests and desires—are. Perhaps even more frequently it is a case where years of on-the-job experience have brought a person to the point that a year or so of special training would mean an enlargement of his or her value.

It is a strange system that makes no provision for the educational renewal opportunities which would give these midcareer decision-points the meaning and significance they ought to have. Nor is there any good or sufficient reason for this. In other comparable countries there are now fairly fully developed arrangements, provided by both practice and law, for promotional leaves of absence for those who have spent some considerable time in the work force. There is precedent elsewhere, too, if there are to be periodic cycles of unemployment, of institutionally arranging for an expansion of educational and training programs during periods of recession and of contracting these programs when the demand for labor increases.

Both the need to extend an education-work policy to the adult years and the promise that such an extension offers become plainer when the particular interests and situations of three large groups—women, racial minorities, and older people—are considered.

We have given little attention to what is actually involved in according women the employment opportunities equal to those of men that they have recently and suddenly been recognized as entitled to. Coming, by no means just coincidentally, with a sharp reduction in the amount of women's time that goes into child-rearing, this presages a vast increase in women's effective demands for jobs previously reserved for men. It also foreshadows, by consequence, a large movement of men off of courses they had previously set for themselves and indeed embarked on. The effect of this will not be confined to changes in entry-level hiring practices. Both among women preparing themselves for different kinds of occupations from those they had originally expected to get into, and among the displaced men moving to something else, there will be substantially increased demands and need for adult education and training programs.

Similar obligations remain to be met as part of the national commitment to end discrimination on account of race. To go behind the superficial statistics sometimes used to show recent gains in the economic and employment circumstances of blacks and other racial minority groups is to encounter grim evidence of what is obvious even without these figures: that meaningful equal employment and earning opportunity depends not only on equal but on compensatory educational opportunity. Providing this only to those members of minority groups who are young is to deny to about 15 million minority adults in this country any significant benefits from an ending of bigotry that was unconscionably long in coming.

In time, too, we must develop in this country an effective political consciousness that will insist, as a matter of equity, on guaranteeing a significant opportunity for educational renewal to the 5 million Americans who "retire" each year, with an average prospect of fifteen years ahead of them. Those years go mostly now into aimless wandering—the consequence of the national misconception that life's ultimate door prize is *security* and that leisure is an unskilled occupation.

There is as strong a case to be made for a year or two of educational renewal opportunity at age sixty as at age sixteen. If it is hard to put the case except in humanistic terms, this is partly because there has been no effort yet to determine, or even to think through, the community value of those services the retired could render if only their obvious capacity to serve were developed.

So far the development of education-work policy has been concerned almost exclusively with the needs of young people for work-related experience as part of their education. A comprehensive policy must accommodate with equal concern the adult's need for periodic redevelopment of skills, capacities, and interests. It may well be that the greatest enlargement of the human resource will come through those educational reforms that would make the opportunity for renewal a citizen's right, supported by law and available as needed throughout one's lifetime. It is as important, in short, to build a significant educational element into the adult, or work, experience as it is to build a larger work element into the youth, or education, experience.

There aren't two worlds—education and work—one for youth, the other for maturity. There is one world—life. No new and sufficient meaning of growth—essential both to the vitality of the system and to the significance of the human experience—will develop from building bridges between schoolroom and employment office. That meaning lies, with whatever power its fuller exploration confirms, in developing a lifetime continuum of education and work opportunities.

How real is this prospect?

The answer will emerge from consideration of two different sets of questions. One of these is about whether such a policy—of interweaving education and work more broadly throughout the life pattern—is sound in itself and consistent with underlying human and national ideals, administratively manageable, economically viable. These are the easier, yet by no means simple, questions.

Idealism doesn't really come into issue. Philosophers, to be sure, reach no consensus about the comparative respect that learning and working and recreating are entitled to or about the ultimate harmony among them. There will always be disagreement, too, about the right mix of general and particularized education at various points in the educational curriculum, and about education's ambivalence as both preparation and end in itself. There will be no significant quarrel, however, with the general proposition that reforming the idea of growth around fuller development and use of the human capacity will yield larger satisfaction from the life experience, which is what idealism is mostly about.

Neither are there any daunting questions here about administrative do-ability. Some of the needs—for adequate guidance and counseling procedures, better manpower requirement and career outlook information, increased attention to work satisfaction, fuller use of available educational technologies—are challenges to good management, but these are in no way forbidding. More meaningful individualization of education will require a higher ratio of teachers and administrators to clients, and flexible and part-time work scheduling will mean management headaches; there are also cost items here to be given account. But there are no limiting factors so far as administrative know-how is concerned. The largest problem here is one of broader governance. Enlisting the community, the public, more fully in the enterprise—and developing broader participation instead of relying so largely on the surrogate of representation—gets into an area in which the art has been to some extent lost. This isn't as easy in a large society as it was in a smaller one. But democracy's boast that government of the people can also be *by* them has never been conditioned on the size of the membership.

The economics of education-work policy present larger questions, partly because they have been so little considered. The immediate reaction to a suggestion involving more of the collective time being spent in education and possibly less (although this isn't clear) in work is "Who will pay for it?" Who picks up the bill for community internships for youth, sabbaticals in midcareer, and renewal as well as security for those who are getting older? Only work is thought of as productive in the support sense, with the measure of any activity's contribution being whether it can be sold at a price and contributes (by that definition) to the national product. The idea of education as a profitable investment for the society, equity financing in effect, is only paid lip service in June commencement speeches. There has been virtually no analysis of the maximally efficient, economic, and high-yield distribution of people's time as between work and education and recreation or leisure—except within the perimeters, and using the parameters, of conventional economic theory. Nobody knows how an econometric model built on an assumption of a vastly enlarged learning industry would work out.

The harder questions, though, about the viability of an education-work policy, are those which turn not on the elements of such a policy itself but on uncertainties about the dynamics of social change in general. Where does the leadership come from for a program of change that involves so many different parts of now rigorously categorized life, reaches this far into rigidly institutionalized structures, disturbs this many comfortable bureaucracies, demands that things be done differently not only at national but perhaps even more at local community levels? How, even more basically, is there to be the mobilization of the society's membership—without which leadership is impotent—that will permit a coalition constituency to develop a working majority in support of what superficially appear to be widely disparate interests?

These are in large part questions about the democratic polity that

reach entirely beyond the limited grasp of this particular consideration. What *is* here is, in significant measure, an expression of faith
that the American ideal is still capable of drawing on its wellspring
and that there is both a desire and a purpose among enough people
that there be this enlargement of education and work—which are
both system forces and human values. This faith is emboldened today
by the perhaps less elevated conviction that there is no alternative to
this course except to enter deliberately upon the decline and the fall of
democratic capitalism's enlightened empire.

There are three critical elements—interrelated but different in
character—of a strategy of change:

First, only a *comprehensive* education-work policy will be
effective—one covering both the improvement of education by a
larger infusion of the instruction of experience and the enrichment of
life's full experience by the opportunity for education's renewal. The
pragmatic consideration here is the necessity of developing a working
majority to support this change.

Second, this comprehensive education-work policy will be most
effectively developed by a careful and deliberate identification of
already established beachheads of consensus regarding particular
programs and then by enlarging these beachheads until a broader
front for larger change can be established.

Third, a meaningful education-work policy can be effective only as
*collaborative processes* are devised to both develop and implement
the program elements of such a policy. The superior opportunity for
this is at the local community level.

What these three elements have in common is that they relate not
just to building better bridges between two worlds, of education and
work, but to integrating these forces in the one world of
community—and life.

# I: Youth

WILLY: I thought I'd go out with my older brother . . . and maybe settle in the North. . . . And I was almost decided to go, when I met a salesman in the Parker House. His name was Dave Singleman. And he was eighty-four years old, and he'd drummed merchandise in thirty-one states. And old Dave, he'd go up to his room, y'understand, put on his green velvet slippers—I'll never forget—and pick up his phone and call the buyers, and without ever leaving his room, at the age of eighty-four, he made his living. *And when I saw that, I realized that selling was the greatest career a man could want.* 'Cause what could be more satisfying than to be able to go, at the age of eighty-four, into twenty or thirty different cities, and pick up a phone, and be remembered and loved and helped by so many different people?

*Death of a Salesman* by Arthur Miller (New York: The Viking Press, 1949).

I was assigned to George, the timber man, a big, paternal old-timer. We went into the shaft, and suddenly the roof was about a yard high. He moved right along, using a hammer as a third leg. . . . I watched him set timbers, under fractured rocks, slabs that might have weighed half a ton each. I learned that I was there in case one fell on him, so that after I made my way back to the main shaft in a week, I could tell somebody about it.

. . . I've watched the men in the hall when we wait for the shift to change. They know they'll be here six days a week, changing shifts every week, until their lungs go or they're seriously maimed. . . . They were kidding each other about how worthless they were to have spent their lives in the pits. They saw by my orange helmet that I was new, and had a lot of fun talking about how worthless I must be to have ended up in the mine.

"Notes from a Coal Mine" by Meade Arble, *New York Times Magazine,* January 12, 1975.

16

I got a job working for a watch repair shop. . . . It didn't pay much, only forty dollars a week. But I didn't need much money. I had all the clothes and stuff I needed, and I was free. . . . I even had the feeling that if I wanted to become a doctor or something like that, I could go on and do it. This was the first time in my life that I'd had that kind of feeling, and getting out of Harlem was the first step toward that freedom.

. . . I just got tired of it one day. I felt I was going to crack up, just blow it. I said, "Look, I'm tired. You take this job; you just take it and shove it," and I walked out of the shop. I didn't know where I was going. I didn't have any money; I didn't have anything, but I couldn't feel too bad about it or the least bit frightened. I was aware that I hadn't had anything all my life. I'd had jobs, money, and expensive clothes, but I still hadn't had anything.

> *Manchild in the Promised Land* by Claude Brown (New York: The Macmillan Company, 1965).

"People look for individuals who resemble them; therefore if you are different (black) you are at a disadvantage if your boss is white, which is the case 99.9 percent of the time."

> Banker, quoted in *Black Managers in White Corporations* by John P. Fernandez (New York: John Wiley & Sons, 1975).

Long silences mean gloom for her, and I comment on it. She looks up and then looks down again.

"It was all those people in the cars coming the other way," she says. "The first one looked so sad. And then the next one looked exactly the same way, and then the next one and the next one, they were all the same."

"They were just commuting to work."

She perceives well but there was nothing unnatural about it. "Well, you know, *work,*" I repeat. "Monday morning. Half asleep. Who goes to work Monday morning with a grin?"

"It's just that they looked so *lost,*" she says. "Like they were all dead. Like a funeral procession."

> *Zen and The Art of Motorcycle Maintenance: An Inquiry Into Values* by Robert M. Pirsig (New York: William Morrow and Company, 1974).

"I graduated from high school (Baltimore) but I don't know anything. I'm dumb. Most of the time I don't even say I graduated, 'cause then somebody asks me a question and I can't answer it, and they think I was lying about graduating. . . . They graduated me but I don't know anything. I had lousy grades but I guess they wanted to get rid of me."

> *Tally's Corner* by Elliott Liebow (New York: Little, Brown and Company, 1967).

# Youth

For Sharon, a college junior living in Chicago, it was a painful decision. She had always wanted to be a fashion designer. But after reviewing her job potential with a B'nai B'rith career counselor, she switched to studying speech pathology.

Ellen ... had already been graduated—magna cum laude—and had received a teacher's certificate. She is working as a receptionist.

Arthur, who lives in the Middle West, isn't working at all. He has a Ph. D., but can't find a job in his field: Linguistics and cultural anthropology. So for now, he is on welfare.

From case files of the B'nai B'rith Career and Counseling Services, as reported by Irving Spiegel in the *New York Times,* January 19, 1975.

"I'm no dummy. I'm going back to school," said Robert Sobus, 20, who has worked 18 months on the GM line "hanging springs" and earning about $240 a week.

"Idle GM Workers Talk About Their Uncertain Futures," *The Washington Post,* January 13, 1975.

# In Brief

Whatever may be the ultimate reach and potential of education-work policy, its significant development currently is in and around the passage between classrooms and what, not realizing its implications, we still call the "labor market." About 4 million young Americans pass this checkpoint each year. In most cases its anticipation has dominated their thinking for several years before that; and the passage won't be thought of as completed for a considerable period thereafter.

This, however, only half suggests the number of people vitally interested in what happens here. To about an equal number of us who are older, it means our ultimate fulfillment or failure—as parents. A more rational school-to-work policy, therefore, will probably develop from institutional leaders and a working majority of the body politic sensing as mothers and fathers a pattern of need and a course of action less clearly discernible in the exercise of our formal responsibilities as officials and citizens.

Consideration of the prospects for an improvement in this situation proceeds properly from the clearest possible recognition of how it stands today, pursuing a course of change helpfully marked out in terms of three overlapping but separately identifiable phases:

First, the need to "do something" is now strongly felt, although in terms (a "20 percent youth unemployment rate," for example) that do little to inform an effective course of action. The thermometer readings confirm the fact of a dangerously high fever but don't identify the reasons for it. A further effort must be made to understand this situation in terms of its elements and its causes. Chapter 1 is an attempt to do this.

Second, a considerable and significant effort has already been made to meet particular manifestations of these difficulties. Large doses of aspirin have been administered. Most of these efforts are superficial, or addressed to apparent emergencies. They reach, at best, only those parts of the problem that are remedial (1) within the school-to-work passage itself, (2) through already established processes, and (3) within the traditional institutional structure.

Yet the initiatives already undertaken are critically important. This stage of research, development, experimentation, and what may be largely improvisation is the essential preliminary to any larger-scale undertaking. It includes what is at least a probing *toward* the more basic causes and the broader answers and gives the future the instruction of trial, resulting in both error and effectiveness. Chapters 2 and 3 identify some six program elements that emerge from these initiatives already undertaken as warranting particular further development; a number of suggestions are made for further advances along these lines.

It has become increasingly apparent, however, that the key to implementation of an effective school-to-work policy is the development of new *processes* through which these various programs can be made more meaningful. These must be *collaborative* processes, involving participation by the schools, the employment community, and the community at large. The largest need, moreover, is for the development of such processes at the *local* level. Toward this end, Chapter 4 proposes the establishment of Community Education-Work Councils.

# 1.
# No Man's —
# or Woman's — Land

Every American over fourteen and going on twenty-one moves through a maze of legal markers and mores reflecting prevailing, often contradictory, views about the relationship of age to capacity: to drive a car, to vote, to marry, to fight a war, to have a credit card, to be or not to be an adult. "Just tell me," your sixteen-year-old interrupts, "how old do I have to be to get into the human race?" You are glad and a little surprised at this continuing interest, and you wish you knew the answer.

This general ambivalence about coming of age shows up in its sharpest form when the time comes to leave school and go to work. Suddenly, after years of acclimation to a compulsory and highly structured school system, young people find themselves almost entirely on their own.

Unhappily, this abrupt change is only a particularly critical incident in a pervasive confusion about how the education and work chapters in people's lives are supposed to fit together. In a great many cases they don't fit at all.

Statistics are boring. They are also dangerous. We use them as mirrors in which to look at ourselves, without realizing that they reflect only those features of the human circumstance that can be quantified. Most of them report only conditions, not causes. If they seem to call for action we start looking for shortcuts, even across quicksand.

There are, though, some figures that—if shaken well before using—tell quite a lot about how badly these education and work processes have gotten out of kilter and about the difficulty and waste this is causing.

The youth unemployment rate in this country is a startling 20 percent, a statistic that is truly meaningful, however, only by comparison.

It is almost three times as high as the rate for adults. It is twice as high as it was when these figures were first collected in 1947. It is up from 12 percent ten years ago. Unemployment among teenagers (sixteen to nineteen) was 15 percent in February 1974 and 19.9 percent in February 1975.

The unemployment rate is twice as high among those who are both young and black or of Mexican, Puerto Rican, or American Indian descent. Among these, the rate now exceeds 40 percent.

In any particular month between a million and a half and 2 million teenagers are looking for work and unable to find it—which is the only circumstance that the current measurement system defines as "unemployed." This means that in the course of a year between 4 and 5 million young people will go through this experience. This is just about half of all of those who look for work during the course of a year.

These youth figures get buried in the monthly reports of the country's *overall* situation. In the minds of most people the picture of unemployment is of a head of a family who loses his or her job; and this indeed is generally the more serious situation. But almost a quarter of all unemployment in the United States is among teenagers. Over a third is among those under twenty-two, although they make up only one seventh of the work force.

This is an intolerable situation. It warrants some very different action from what the rest of the unemployment picture calls for. We have simply got to pay attention to it.

But figuring out what to do requires some further understanding of what these figures really mean and taking into account quite a lot of other information as well. Indeed these youth unemployment rates, standing alone, come very close to being, in Cervantes' phrase, facts that are enemies to the truth. There isn't any question about their accuracy. They have been checked and cross-checked and honed to seasonally adjusted, decimal-point precision. What they say is true. But what they say is in some substantial respects different from what people generally *understand* them to say; and the conditioned response they evoke—that the answer here is just "more jobs"— is dangerously wrong.

A few for instances:

John A and Mary B are high school graduates who have had all the school they want for right now, are willing and able to work, and are looking for jobs but can't find them. Their situations may leave questions about what their abilities and desires and prospects would be if they had had different schooling or different backgrounds, and there is the question, too, of the likelihood—now that machines have virtually the equivalent of high school educations—of young A and B "ever amounting to much." These though, at least in current terminology, are properly classified as cases of "unemployment." Yet less than a quarter of that reported 20 percent involves the John As and Mary Bs.

Henry C and Robert D are seniors in high school, both doing well, and looking forward to college. They try to get work after school, on weekends, or during holidays. C wants money to keep up his car; with D it is a matter of being able or unable to stay in school. But there are no part-time jobs to be found. Are C and D properly reported among the country's "unemployed"—along with forty-year-old heads of households? Are the C and D cases enough alike to be measured together? In any event, about half those officially reported as unemployed among sixteen-to-nineteen-year-olds are in school and looking only for part-time employment.

Helen E and William F dropped out after two years of high school, have had three or four jobs they couldn't or at least didn't hold, and are looking again. Unemployed? Yes, but with the obviously serious question of whether "more jobs" is the answer to their problem. And theirs is the situation that prevails for most of the rest of that 20 percent.[1]

Susan G and Robert H have finished high school and are in their first year at college. They despise every minute of it and are only going through the motions of learning. They want very much to get out, and probably will. The only figures they show up in are those for college enrollments, the rise in which we cheer, no questions asked.

Finally, Philip I, Frances J, and Eileen K, have all left school—one without a high school diploma and by economic necessity, another on graduating and by choice, the third when she failed college in her freshman year. They all looked for work, found it, and are staying with it. But they are in jobs that, in themselves, lead nowhere. These three—and unnumbered hundreds of thousands like them—are presently carried on the credit side of the ledger, as employed.

In short, these youth "unemployment rate" figures—based on concepts developed essentially to measure the adult work situation—reflect poorly what is, in fact, only one aspect of a basic change in the ways young people are spending their transitional years: They are now both in school *and* working.

The two parts of this picture are closely interrelated. To see the whole, it is essential to look at some of the education figures for these same youth, to consider their enrollment and unenrollment as well as their employment and unemployment.

For the past two decades the American education system has been struggling valiantly to cope with an increased demand for its product. The demand has gone up for two reasons: an unprecedented increase in the number of school-age youth in the population as a result of the postwar baby boom,[2] and a significant strengthening of the country's commitment to send as many of its younger members as possible through elementary school, high school, and on to college.[3]

At least by quantitative measure, the system has performed well. Between the school years 1953-1954 and 1969-1970, enrollment in elementary schools increased by more than 9 million (41.6 percent), in secondary schools by more than 6.5 million (112 percent), and at the higher educational level by about 6 million (250 percent).[4] Since these increases in enrollments during the sixteen years outpaced increases in the size of these population groups, *un*enrollment rates went down significantly.

Nevertheless, large numbers of young people remain unenrolled. A recent astonishing report, still neither explained nor fully verified, is that 2 million boys and girls between seven and seventeen are, for one reason or another, not in school.[5] One out of every ten in the sixteen-to-seventeen-year-old age group has dropped out or been pushed out.[6] Under today's circumstance, this spells trouble, both for the individual and for the rest of us. If a high school diploma is no longer a significant job credential—and it isn't—and if a surprising number of high school age youth aren't even in school, it hardly seems to be ground for optimism that half of all high school graduates now go on to college.

So there is going to have to be continuing attention to the fact that a lot of young people are still leaving school without passports to any place. Who are they? Why are they leaving? What happens to them?

Only beginning efforts have been made to get at the information that will answer these questions. The answers will come only from longitudinal studies—which go into the backgrounds of particular groups of young people of the same age and then follow them not only through their school years but their subsequent experience. One such study, initiated at the University of Michigan in 1966, has already yielded significant enlightenment: Dropping out of high school is better recognized not as a problem in itself but as a symptom of *other* problems rooted in family and economic background, ability limitations, and difficulties in school. As much of this often traces to institutional shortcomings as to individual fault.[7]

One significant element in the recent record of changing school enrollments at various age levels is that previous racial differences have been notably reduced and almost eliminated.[8] This is true, at the postsecondary level, to a considerable but lesser extent of sex differences. Fifty-three percent of 1972 male high school graduates went on to college, compared with 46 percent of the female graduates. Ten years earlier the respective figures were 55 and 43 percent.

A good deal of speculation circulates about the causes of the decrease, during this ten-year period, in the percentage of male high school graduates going on to college, some of it bearing directly on the education-work relationship. But a simple comparison of the 1962 and 1972 figures obscures what could be an even more telling fact—that the 1962 rate of 55 percent had risen to 63 percent by 1968, before dropping sharply to the 1972 level of 53 percent. Possible causes have been summarized recently in the Department of Labor (Bureau of Labor Statistics) publication on "The High School Class of 1972"[9]:

Undoubtedly, lessened pressure to go to college to avoid the draft is one. Another factor may be disillusionment over the prospects of obtaining a good job after graduation, in light of the increase in unemployment in recent years among new college graduates. The rising costs of college tuition and other school-related expenses may be a bar to some youths. Still another influence may also have been the increasing number of young people who take time out between high school and college to work, travel, or otherwise try a change of pace.

By their apparent consistency, enrollment statistics contribute on the whole to an illusion that the pattern of education is now set in this country. It obviously is not. The figures reflect too little the impact during the past decade of the postwar baby boom as its reverbera- tions have moved through the educational system. Moreover, they show only the beginning effects of the country's acceptance, in principle, of the equal-opportunities standard for both women and minority groups. And these are all only head-count figures. This much, though, is clear: More and more young people are going to be staying longer and longer in one form of institutionalized education or another.

Why, then, with educational enrollment figures going up so dramatically, is there at the same time such a sharp increase in the unemployment rates among the same group of people? More in school, more out of work. It doesn't seem to make sense.

And it doesn't. There is an imperative need to be met here. The apparent anomaly develops from looking at the education and work figures separately. Both to clear it up and, much more significantly, to get on with meeting this imperative need, the two pictures must be put together.

The Bureau of Labor Statistics now reports that almost 40 percent of sixteen-to-nineteen-year-old boys and girls who are in school are also either working or looking for work, in most cases part-time jobs. This report is based on monthly interviews with parents drawn from a national sample of household surveys. Interestingly, a survey based on interviews with young people themselves shows even more work activity among those in school—at percentages between 50 percent and 60 percent, depending largely on age and race.[10]

These current, or very recent, figures are markedly higher, especially for girls, than they were ten and fifteen years ago. Thirty-nine percent of all sixteen-to-seventeen-year-old boys in school in 1970 were also in the work force (that is, either working or looking for work; up from 34 percent in 1960. Among eighteen- and nineteen-year-old boys, the 1970 figure was 41 percent, up from 35 percent. The increases among girls have been even larger: up from 23 percent in 1960 to 34 percent in 1970 for sixteen-to-seventeen-year-olds, and from 28 percent to 38 percent for eighteen-to-nineteen year-olds.[11]

This increased "starlighting"—going to school and working (or trying to) at the same time—is significant in several respects. It is part of the reason the youth unemployment rate is as high as it is. The larger number of marginally qualified workers—those who move in and out of the "labor market" as holidays and vacations and school pressures come and go, who look for part-time work that can be fitted into what are primarily school schedules—is bound to create more situations in which the work being looked for can't be found.

In this connection serious question arises whether the sixteen-to-nineteen-year age group should be included at all in the overall national employment and unemployment figures. These figures used to include fourteen- and fifteen-year-olds as well, but they were removed with publication of data for 1967, and there would appear to be as much reason today for excluding at least the sixteen-to-seventeen-year-old group. The adult unemployment situation is so essentially different from the typical youth unemployment situation—especially in the case of students in schools—that the records should probably be segregated. This would concentrate *separate* attention on the youth unemployment situation, with its much higher figures, thus better illuminating the essentially different problems it presents and facilitating efforts to work out the different answers it requires.

The more basic implication of this increased "starlighting" is that there is already in place a broad base for the development of the work-study and experiential learning programs that are now the subject of so much increased attention among educators. It is time to recognize this subject, and to approach it, as a matter of *both* education and work. What these young people are telling us, by what they are already doing, is that we are making a serious mistake in keeping two separate sets of books and virtually ignoring this now substantial area of dual activity simply because the two parts of it come under the different institutional jurisdictions.

Looked at all together with both eyes instead of separately with one eye on each, these statistics show some other things—four in particular—that must be taken into account before the education and work gears can be properly meshed:

1. A substantial number of these high school and college students who are looking for work *are* finding it. Their difficulties in finding work are often substantial enough to get them into the unemployment statistics as now collected; but in one way or another, at one time or another, a lot of them are getting work experience of some kind or other. This does *not* make the work-study and experiential learning initiatives less important. On the contrary. What it indicates is that with perhaps only minimal collaborative administration, this catch-as-catch-can starlighting could probably be made into a much more effective, and certainly more efficient, school-to-work operation.

Youth *employment* is increasing significantly—that is, it was, until the recent worsening of the economy. Between 1960 and 1970 it rose by 49 percent, exceeding the 41 percent increase in the teenage population and greatly exceeding the 20 percent increase in total employment.[12]

In October 1973, when this situation was most recently surveyed, the number of teenagers (sixteen-to-nineteen-years-old) *in school and employed* was 3.8 million. This is only about one third of them.[13] But this is during a single school month. When the fact of larger youth employment during the summer months and certain holiday months

27

is taken into account, along with the fact that different young people are employed at different times during the year, it appears that about half of all sixteen-to-nineteen-year-olds who are in school are also getting *some* outside employment during the course of the year.

Some other incomplete figures tend to confirm what these BLS reports suggest: *that in the course of what is primarily their school experience, three out of every four young people are getting some kind of actual work experience in the competitive labor market.* This does *not* satisfy the necessity of including a broad experiential learning component in the educational curriculum; what it *does* suggest strongly is that unless whatever is going on now in the economy disrupts this so far encouraging development, the makings of such a component are available.

2. The work young people are doing—both those who are still students and those who have left school—is taking on a distinctive character of its own.

There is increasing talk and evidence of the emergence of still undefined youth-type jobs. This does *not*, however, mean dead-end jobs.

Teenage employment today is concentrated in a band of unskilled jobs. The relative importance of this fact is shown clearly when compared to the proportion of similar jobs held by older males with the *same education*. Among eighteen- and nineteen-year-olds, 58 percent were nonfarm laborers or operatives in 1969, whereas only 27 percent of males age twenty-five to forty-four were in these same occupations.[14] Other figures show no significant differences (at least among males) in the occupational distribution of eighteen- and nineteen-year-olds as between out-of-school youth with high school diplomas and those without.[15] Although this occupational concentration of youth employment is nothing new, it is showing up more and more sharply.

It is increasingly evident, beyond this, that private employers, particularly the larger corporations, are hiring fewer and fewer males under age twenty for what are normally considered "entry-type jobs with a prospect of upward mobility."[16] This is true even with respect to jobs traditionally considered as requiring no more than a high school education to perform. (The surveys made so far include hotel clerks, arc welders, bank tellers, hospital orderlies, and so on.) No distinction is being made between those with and those without high school diplomas.[17]

On the other hand, the available statistics disclose striking differences in the kinds of jobs female high school graduates are able to get. Both graduates and nongrads are heavily concentrated in traditional "female" occupations. Yet 60 percent of the employed female graduates (eighteen- and nineteen-years-old) are, for example, in clerical occupations, as compared to only 25 percent of the nongrads.[18] So far as this "transitional" period is concerned, young women entering employment directly out of high school, unlike young men following the same route, get jobs of a similar nature to those held by adult women who have been in the labor force for some time. This is a reflection of the limited range of employment opportunities available for women in general—regardless of age or educational and experiential backgrounds. The short of it is that women are put in their place sooner rather than later.

3. It is in a sense only a different aspect of the preceding point that there is a critical change going on in the ratio between the number of young people getting more education and the number of jobs presumed to require higher levels of education.

In 1970 about one in six members of the adult labor force had only an elementary education or less. This will decline precipitiously to *one in sixteen* by 1990. At the other end, one in eight had four years of college or more in 1970; by 1990 college education is projected to spread to the point where about one out of every four citizens will be a degree holder.[19] Optimism for the educational requirements of jobs keeping pace has little basis in the trends of the past several decades, a matter discussed in some detail in Chapter 5.

4. It is *apparently* true that more and more young people are orienting their education and training toward *particular* occupational and career prospects, but that fewer of them are finding, when they are through, the jobs they had prepared for.

The clearest current illustration of this mismatch is in the report that 4 million elementary and secondary teachers will have been trained during the present decade for what will be only 2 million openings. The announcement of a single opening in the English department in a small New England college recently brought more than 1200 applications. Young people with unquestionable qualifications in a variety of areas look futilely for jobs today—while the help wanted columns in the newspapers list more and more needs for computer programmers.

This subject warrants further development. It is by no means clear that more sharply oriented education is less valuable than a general course of study, even if the particular opportunity prepared for turns out not to be available. There are some other things to be considered.

It is, however, critically important that the development of skills be better matched with society's needs for these skills. So far we lack the facts necessary either to understand the seeming mismatch or to correct it.

Give me, Richelieu boasted, six sentences from the words of the most innocent of men, and I will hang him with them. So it is, too, of statistics, which can serve opposite conclusions equally well, depending on who makes the selection from among them. These seem, however, to be the facts in the education-work records that are the closest allies to the truth:

- Whatever may be its various interpretations, the 20 percent youth unemployment rate—40 percent for those doubly disadvantaged by age and descent—*demands* attention to this youth problem.
- The education and work elements in the youth situation cannot responsibly be considered separately; most of these young people at and approaching this critical transition point are both in school and in the work force.
- More and more of them are getting more and more education and mixing it with more and more work experience.
- There *is* work to be done by youth; it is emerging increasingly as work with particular characteristics—distinguishing it in material respects from the work that most adults do.
- The rising "educational attainment level of the work force" has a significant impact on what an education-work policy should be.
- There is evidence of an increasing mismatch between the development of particular competencies and the need for them, but the evidence regarding this is inadequate and the analysis incomplete.
- The answer is not just more school and more jobs for everybody under twenty, if what this means is simply staying longer in the same old classrooms and then looking for some work to relieve the extended monotony of it.

The prevailing mood today is a compound of national exasperation with somebody else and frustration at our own failures. Much of public commentary seems to have become a more-apocalyptic-than-thou kind of sweepstakes. We are down in the mouth and inclined to be perhaps overly self-critical.

But we don't like it this way, and there is no point or reason in approaching this education work situation in negative, overly critical terms.

30

The shock that most youth unquestionably experience during the critical initiation rite they go through as they move from learning to earning 'a living is a result neither of neglect nor of any deliberate intent to toughen up the young. It is the consequence, rather, of a giant society's always lumbering and awkward movement in reshaping its traditional processes and its established institutional structures to the impetuous imperatives of change.

It would be worse error to suggest or imply that the passage from youth to adulthood used to be something that was either easily or satisfactorily accomplished, and that this has now some way gone wrong. No boy or girl in this country today, knowing even a little of history, would trade present circumstances or prospects for those any earlier time afforded—or for those currently available any place else in the world.

That, though, isn't the question. The essential quality of this country's remarkable progress in the past decade and a half is that we no longer measure where we are by where we used to be, but rather by where we now know we can go. Part of this current sense of frustration is from our own revolution of increased expectations— and from a new realization that the improvement of the human condition is so much more within the human competence than we used to think. So we look today from a higher vantage point—in a wider perspective of larger purpose—at the manifest evidence of serious losses and costs being incurred at the transfer point between education and work.

# 2.
# "New Ways..."

In late August 1974 a new President, having taken office only a few days before at a time of incredible national disorder, made a commencement address at Ohio State University. He took as his subject a matter so totally removed from the national obsession of the moment that his attention to it was more than a little wondered at. He had chosen to talk about the relationship, more particularly the breakdown in the relationship, between education and work.

From the way he put what he said that day, it was conjectured that Gerald Ford was speaking not only as President but equally as parent. "The time has come for a fusion of the realities of work-a-day life with the teaching of academic institutions." He asked that common counsel be taken about "new ways to bring the world of work and the institutions of education closer together."

New ways? What could this mean in an area characterized for the past decade by such a multiplication of work-study, cooperative education, experiential learning, and career education proposals, by such a plethora of initiatives, pilot projects, experiments, and innovations that every possibility of novelty must surely have been already exhausted?

Yet the request for new ways was unquestionably apt. It was, it seems fair to infer, a request for two things:

First, for a consolidation now of what has been a richness of experience but a poverty of accomplishment; a selection of those *program elements* that emerge from this experience as offering, given the encouragement of a President's conviction, the largest promise of improvement in the present condition.

And second, for the identification of the *process elements* in a strategy of change that will give these program proposals the force in action they have had, so far, only in principle.

Looking back over the decade, and leaving the "process" point for later consideration, it is clear that there are at least six program areas in which answers to the President's request can be found:

1. A more reliable system can be established for identifying the "manpower" needs and career prospects for which education is considered, at least in part, preparation.
2. Present career guidance and counseling and youth job placement functions can be significantly improved.
3. The "career education" concept—infusing the general education process with various forms of exposure to the meaning of work and service—could be developed more fully.
4. Actual work or service experience can be made an integral part of youth's education.
5. Provision can be made for facilitating young people's moving out of the educational sequence and then back into it when their particular circumstances warrant.
6. Present barriers in both law and custom to work or service experience as part of youth's preparation can be removed where they are known to have outlived their original purpose.

"New ways?" Yes, in the sense, as Mr. Justice Holmes once put it, that in these areas "opposite convictions have now long enough kept a battlefront against each other that the notions destined to prevail are now entitled to the field."

## IDENTIFYING "MANPOWER" NEEDS
## AND CAREER PROSPECTS

To begin with, the fusion President Ford spoke of depends on knowing what the "realities of work-a-day life" relevant to the "teaching of academic institutions" actually are.

Identifying both present and prospective "manpower needs" and "occupational outlooks" is familiar business. There has been, though, both uncertainty about how far this can be done as a practical matter and a considerable ambivalence about the necessity, even the desirability, of pushing this possibility to its limits.

There are no longer any doubts about the policy considerations.

Too many young people are unquestionably being educated and trained for prospects that subsequently turn out to be illusions. Other kinds of employment go, at least to some extent, begging. If, furthermore, it develops that the *total* needs in present prospect don't come up to the total supply in the education pipeline, then arrangements are going to have to be made for other uses of the human resource. We need and want whatever facts can be reliably developed.

It is now equally clear that the techniques are available for significantly enlarging the present information base. Quite a lot has already been done toward developing this—more in fact than is currently put to full use. The *Occupational Outlook Handbook,* prepared and published by the Bureau of Labor Statistics, includes a good deal of information about what occupations are like and what is going to happen to them. It reflects in its present form, an increasing sophistication in making projections about the number of jobs in an occupation—and, to a significantly lesser extent, the number of competitors for those jobs. There are instances, of course, where better local use is made of what is available. For instance, in Atlanta, an Occupational Information Center for Education-Industry has been set up to (1) develop work-experience opportunities, (2) provide information to students and counselors on various entry-level jobs available in the metropolitan area, and (3) disseminate facts about the location of job opportunities and the skills necessary to qualify for them. Part of the Atlanta Public School System, the Center acts as a liaison between the schools and employers, working closely with the Superintendent's Office and the Chamber of Commerce.

Three principal weaknesses appear in the present occupational information system. First, there are the inherent limitations on any projections. A shift in attitudes among high school and college students about desirable occupations can throw off the projections of "supply." On the demand side, shifts in the economy or technological breakthroughs will precipitate declines in some kinds of employment, expansions in others. The projections themselves inevitably influence decisions and thereby change the picture.

Second, although the largest usefulness is in local or regional data, most of the available information is only for the nation as a whole. This is particularly unfortunate for the noncollege bound, whose prospects are more likely to be limited to what is available in the area in which they have gone to school. Unfortunately, local information and projections of the same quality as those available for the country as a whole are expensive unless these costs are weighed against the savings such knowledge would yield. In recent years the BLS has developed methods that permit national projections of employment to be adjusted to aggregates for states as a whole.[1] To date approximately forty states have made projections using these methods, and new projections will soon be made for all the states. However, the variation in employment trends for specific occupations may be as great within many states, or nearly as great, as the variation among states.

Not only is information about the future generally unavailable in terms of where people live, information about the present is not sufficiently available either. In most areas the Employment Service Job Banks, developed entirely on the basis of employer requests to the service, contain very few job vacancies for youths. The information about current levels of employment is available locally for specific occupations only for the ten-year interval of the census, so recent trends in employment levels cannot be ascertained. Even the descriptions of what jobs have to offer are presently not adjusted to local areas. After overcoming many obstacles, the Labor Department assembled information on current job vacancies for manufacturing industries in forty-one metropolitan areas, and rather than moving forward, dropped the whole effort.

Third, the availability of good projections doesn't mean they will get to the attention of the student trying to make up his or her mind. There are serious failures of communiction or more broadly of use and implementation.

What, then, are the "new ways" to approach this problem?

To a considerable extent the problem is technical, involving survey and statistical methodologies, and has accordingly been left for its detailed development to a separate monograph prepared as part of · the present project. There are in general, however, five separately identifiable possibilities for significant improvement here.

First, so far as the measurement of manpower needs (the "demand" side of this equation) is concerned, there are several critical requirements, particularly when it comes to the projection of prospective needs: (1) the establishment of a standard occupational classification system; (2) the breaking down of present manpower need measurements into terms of these occupational classificatons; and (3) the further organization of this occupational data on an industry-by-industry basis. The technical basis for doing all of this has been fully developed. Enough additional expense is involved to have been a deterrent, but the costs are not large; they are, in fact, insignificant compared to the savings the changes would bring. Any effective projection of future manpower needs depends on establishing this industry-by-industry occupational data base.

Second, on the "supply" side, there is the inexplicable fact that we don't know how many people in this country are preparing themselves for what occupations (except in the professional fields). The best estimate is that *about* 5 million people complete educational and training courses each year. To go behind this rough figure is to discover that it may be either high or low by as much as 20 percent, and that there is no reliable breakdown (again with the exception of the professions) on an occupational basis. Yet without this information, no real manpower planning or career planning is possible.

Part of the irony of this situation is that most of the *pieces* of this information are already being collected, but by five or six different government agencies with no provision for putting the pieces together. Given the exercise of some centralized authority it would be relatively simple to prepare and maintain a profile of the training force in this country as complete as the presently available picture of the work force. The expense involved would be minimal, the advantage inestimable.

Third, both the demand and the supply information must be developed on a *local,* as well as nationwide, basis. This could be done to a substantial extent—at least so far as the 150 largest metropolitan areas in the country are concerned—by enlarging to about 60,000 the present 46,000 household survey sample used by the Bureau of the Census in its monthly collection of employment and unemployment data. The cost of this expansion is estimated at something less than $5 million a year.

Fourth, there is an essential need for further information about the comparative effectiveness of different combinations of general education and more particularized training courses in various occupational areas. Most young people's career development now includes a combination of two of more kinds of training (general education, public or private specialized training at either the secondary or postsecondary level, on-the-job training, and so forth). The interest of the individual in knowing more about the effectiveness of various possible combinations of such courses is matched by the public interest in determining the cost effectiveness of these different combinations.

The key to the development of this kind of information is the establishment of a much broader system of longitudinal studies in which selected cohorts of young people are identified at early stages in their preparatory programs and then followed on through their education and training and at least the early stages of their subsequent experience. The unquestionably large costs involved here can be substantially reduced—although at some loss in effectiveness—by making these longitudinal studies on a retroactive instead of a follow-through basis, using presently available Social Security data.

It is obviously essential, finally, that these various kinds of information be fully communicated to educational administrators and teachers, and especially to students. The first part of this is easy, involving only the simplest administrative procedures. It will be much harder to get the information into the hands of students, who need it the most.

What, then are the "new ways" to develop an adequate manpower need and career-outlook information base?

• Put the reporting and projecting of manpower needs on an industry-by-industry standard occupational classification basis.

• Survey and report the training force as fully as the work force is presently surveyed and reported.

• Enlarge the Bureau of the Census household survey sample sufficiently (by about 15,000 households) to provide reliable local data, at least in the largest metropolitan areas.

• Determine, through longitudinal studies, the comparative cost effectiveness of various combinations of education and training courses for different kinds of career prospects.

• Develop an adequate communication system to get this information to those who can use it.

CAREER GUIDANCE AND COUNSELING:

YOUTH JOB PLACEMENT

Guidance and counseling and job placement are conventionally treated, in the consideration of the youth problem, as separate and distinct functions. This is the consequence, however, less of any fundamental difference in their nature than of the evolution of their institutionalization: the counseling function as part of the schools' responsibility, job placement as that of the Federal-State Employment Service.

The influence of institutionalism's force goes even deeper. Counseling and guidance first came to be included in the secondary schools' responsibilities almost entirely for the purpose of providing assistance to those high school students going on to college. When it began to be realized, comparatively recently, that a similar service ought to be provided those students who go directly from high school to work, the easiest thing to do was simply to add this to the duties of those who were already providing the advice and information regarding the move from one level of education to another. School-to-work guidance and counseling started out as an orphan function put on an already busy doorstep. It still is.

The story of youth job placement has followed similar but less clear-cut lines. The Federal-State Employment Service, set up under the Wagner-Peyser Act of 1933, became, over the years, a system administered through some 30,000 employees in about 2400 offices established throughout the country. Its principal function—although it occasionally instituted special initiatives directed at youth employment—has always been to help adults who have lost their jobs and to help employers fill vacancies for adult workers. With the recent emergence of public interest in the youth unemployment situation, the almost exclusive reaction has been to leave youth job placement to the Employment Service, where it has been accepted as no better than an unwanted child.

So the superior force of institutional habit has had its victories over good sense. Proposals for "new ways" to fuse workaday realities and academic processes must, therefore, include consideration not only of (1) how to provide high school age students with going-to-work counseling at least as effective as the traditional going-to-college counseling, and (2) how to give youth job placement at least as much attention as adult job placement, but (3) how to combine these youth counseling and job-placement functions regardless of the minor earthquakes doing so will cause in stratified established bureaucracies.

The historical development of these two functions requires that they first be looked at separately.

Guidance and counseling as exercised today at the high school level is by virtually common consent the weakest link in any of the present bridges between the worlds of education and work. Most of those who try to cross these bridges without going by way of college— roughly half of today's youth—do so in virtual ignorance of where they are going, at least so far as any formal guidance is concerned. Those who need such guidance most are getting the least of it.

This is not properly expressed as criticism of professional guidance personnel. What has happened here is that a function previously exercised largely within one institution, the family, has been turned over to another, the schools, without establishing a competence even remotely commensurate with the responsibility involved. The guidance and counseling profession in this country has now grown to ten times the size it was twenty years ago.[2] But as impressive as this figure may appear on its face, it is essentially meaningless for it says nothing of the relationship of personnel to function.

Any rational comprehension of this situation starts from the existing evidence of the ratio today of counselors to students. What figures there are indicate a counselor-student ratio, at the secondary level, of about 1-300 or 400, varying greatly even among major cities; from 1-to-148 in San Diego to 1-to-1200 in New York City.[3] What these figures leave out is that it is almost universal practice to include in the counselors' duties a good many of the high school chores—monitoring hallways while teachers are in the classrooms, handling disciplinary problems, pursuing truants, and so forth—to an estimated extent of about 60 percent of their time.[4]

The most careful calculation from available data is that there is provided today in the American high schools an average of about one person-year of professional counseling time for every 1000 students, most of it going into on-to-college counseling.[5] This leaves out the very considerable time *other* high school teachers spend in what is essentially counseling and guidance. Still, to rely on presently designated guidance and counseling personnel is to assume miracles of loaves and fishes as a daily performance across the country.

To suggest enlargement of this professional corps is hardly thinking in terms of "new ways." And part of the irony of the present situation is that it has gotten so bad that there simply will not be, as a practical matter, significant public support for doing more of the same thing in the same old way.

There would be nothing new, either, in listing for fuller consideration particular counseling and guidance techniques of promising potential: the more extensive use of computers and multimedia materials, a larger reliance on peer-group procedures, or an increased emphasis on the fuller development of self-awareness and confidence in decision-making. A comprehensive catalog of these possibilities is contained in the Career Guidance and Counseling Act, drafted by the American Personnel and Guidance Association and introduced in both Houses of Congress in early 1975. These improvements are important, and serious review of the principles embodied in this proposal is simply elementary good sense.

To be pressed for "new ways," however, is necessarily to push this consideration further along several possible avenues:

There has simply got to be introduced into the career guidance and counseling process a larger knowledge and understanding of what the world of work is and is all about. The 1975 legislative proposal recognizes this but in terms that seem unduly restrained by convention.

The need here is only partly for the kind of manpower and career outlook data discussed in the preceding section, although this is vital. An essential element of good occupational information is a reservoir of honest, accurate descriptions of the nature of the work, including where specific jobs might lead in the future. This material should be prepared in forms directly accessible to students, rather than as reference works for the counselor. Moreover, it should be developed at comprehension and interest levels appropriate for junior high school students[6] as well as for upper teenagers, and especially for youth who may be disadvantaged both by lesser reading facility and a lesser range of occupational choice. (The Bureau of Labor Statistics is currently engaged in developmental work on occupational information specifically for such youth.)[7]

It is probably more important that there also be included substantial opportunity for students to get a *firsthand* exposure to people with actual experience in this other world—as they do, incidentally, in their on-to-college counseling; every counselor carries an academic degree. This means questioning very seriously, indeed it means changing, the present credentialing practices of the counseling profession and recognizing the desirability of including in the counseling corps individuals with other than academic experience. Or it means requiring that all, or at least substantial numbers, of counselors have such other experience to a significant degree. A recent change in New York in the traditional credentialing requirements presages the opening up of the counseling function to any person with substantial experience who has undergone appropriate preparation.

This need also commends strongly that it be identified as part of the proper discharge of the counselors' function to make use in this process of the virtually limitless supply in most communities of volunteers—people with work experience of various kinds (including personnel work in various industries and occupations) who would be glad to put themselves and their experience at the counselors' and the students' disposal. This cuts across another professional prejudice by no means limited to the counseling profession: reliance on voluntarism. But so far at least as the occupational information part of career counseling is concerned, that prejudice simply has to be set aside. The maximally effective use of a large part of a high school counselor's time under present typical circumstances would probably be in the marshaling of other community counseling resources.

There is a further dimension of the point that underlies the preceding suggestions. Can a function that involves so much of necessary familiarity with two worlds be effectively based, in institutional terms, entirely in one of those worlds? In terms of organizational necessities, there may be no practical alternative. Counseling is, will probably remain, and very possibly should be, part of the education system. It will be considered in Chapter 4, however, whether there are additional processes that could be developed to take fuller account of the special two-world quality of this particular function.

There is, finally, the related question of whether there is some way—and whether it is desirable—to develop the role of the counselor so that it includes at least some measure of particular representation *of the youth* in dealing with the "establishment," rather than as another representative of the establishment in dealing with the youth.

Looking back over the American story, one sees a shifting from time to time about the whole idea of young people working, and consequently about the question of where the responsibility lies for providing whatever institutional help is to be given them—by the family, the schools, or the public employment agencies—in finding jobs when the time for that comes. This has all developed very naturally and, on the whole, from what is unquestionably a deep concern for youth's "getting a good start in the world." Almost ironically, however, the changing pattern of this history has contributed to what is today almost a vacuum of institutional responsibility.

The family's role in this process—originally so pervasive that children took their names from their fathers' trades (Mason, Farmer, Carpenter, Miller, Smith), and only a little less so when the customary pattern was to stay on the land or do usually about what their parents had done—has slowly but constantly eroded for a variety of reasons. Today the role of the family seems almost negligible, although this is in some ways and to an extent an illusion.

With the development of compulsory education and then the introduction of child labor laws—and a gradual extension of the idea of a public interest in children's staying longer in school and not going to work too early—the concept of public responsibility for job placement also developed. This was never, at least until recently, at all clearly identified with the schools, although there have always been traces in the school-student relationship of a sense of obligation. When the U.S. Employment Service was set up more than forty years ago, the authorizing act made specific reference to the employment of youth. Yet, historically USES has given only occasional emphasis to youth job placement.

Over the years public concern has shifted from preventing the too-early employment of children to seeing to it that they find work when they are ready for it. The net of it today is that nobody is in charge. The most serious consequence, moreover, is that the least help is provided those who need it most and whom the public has the largest interest in seeing get it. It is a strange and never intended situation that tens of thousands of public dollars will be invested in providing one young person with years of higher preparatory education, and so little will be put into seeing what can be done about another's moving directly from high school to work. In no sense has this developed retributively. It's just bad business to which attention is now, belatedly, being given.

Although the Wagner-Peyser Act was adopted in 1933, it was not until 1950 that a formal Employment Service program for youth was begun—a cooperative program with public schools. At best, it was a one-shot service; Employment Service personnel came to the school, registered seniors not going on to college for job placement, and perhaps offered a series of tests and a counseling interview. The number of high schools involved grew impressively, to the point that by 1962 some service was available in 47 percent of the schools. During that year the program was credited with the actual placement of a modest 113,000. A peak figure of over 1.8 million placements of *all* persons under twenty-two years of age was reported for 1966.

Those figures offer, however, illusory encouragement. They have, for one thing, declined sharply in recent years. The reporting system was corrected in 1970 to record individuals (a significantly lower number) instead of placements. By 1972 the estimate was that 800,000 individuals under age twenty-two were placed by the service. But most of these are in the twenty-or-over age bracket.[8] No figures are available for the particularly critical teenage group; very few of them get jobs through the Employment Service.

The available evidence indicates that only about one out of six teenagers (sixteen to nineteen) looking for work even goes to the Employment Service. Among those who are employed, only about 3 percent surveyed in January 1973 credit the Employment Service with directing them to their present jobs. The overwhelming percentage of jobs obtained are found through friends or relatives (30 percent) or by going to the employer directly and independently (33 percent). Eight percent get their jobs through want-ads, only 7 percent through school placement offices or teachers, and only 3 percent through private employment agencies.[9]

Where placement by the public agency is made, there is no regular follow-up that would make evaluation of the quality of placements possible. The failure to keep in touch with young workers and make sure that their jobs are working out well is one aspect of the general lack of resources and commitment to a high-quality placement service for youth. (In Japan, by contrast, where the unemployment rate for young workers is much lower than in the United States, the public employment service follows up young workers for several years and often finds other jobs for those whose initial placement was not successful.)

In some 100 cities the Employment Service offices also now supply schools and other interested institutions with daily computer printouts of the local job bank data. But this includes only that information that comes from job orders filed by local employers; and most employers don't use the Employment Service to recruit teenage employees except for a few limited types of jobs.

Turning to the schools' role in youth job placement, there have been two lines of development that diverged sharply for a time but are now drawing back together. The reaction in the public high schools, as the concern about youth unemployment increased during the 1960s, was to draw back from the job placement responsibility completely. They already had more to do than they could handle. The counselors continued their college placement mission but accepted beyond that only a nebulous area of responsibility for the development of self-awareness and at most a very general exposure to what work might look like in the pages of the *Occupational Outlook Handbook*. Job placement was marked, quite understandably, as somebody else's business.

There has been a very different attitude, though, in the technical high schools and in the two-year colleges that grew so in number and size during the last decade, and particularly in the private proprietary trade and technical schools. All, or at least the better of these, have given serious attention to the placement of those who finish their courses. Unquestionably, this is part of their increasing attraction to

43

young people and probably, as the carrot replaces the stick in learning's dynamics, an important part of their pedagogy.

What about "new ways," then, for improving youth job placement? What seems most worth consideration is the need to clarify what the relationship is to be between this and guidance and counseling and then to decide where the institutional responsibility is to be placed— so that it will no longer be lost in the cracks.

In the Education Amendments of 1972, the Congress mandated the Commissioner of Education (in the Office of Education of the Department of Health, Education, and Welfare) to: "promote and encourage occupational preparation, counseling and guidance, and job placement or placement in post-secondary education programs as a responsibility of elementary and secondary schools." This makes imperative now the exercise of executive responsibility to coordinate and integrate what have operated too long as separate institutional systems. This can be accomplished only at the *top* executive levels in both the federal and the state governments. There is ample executive authority to do this, although more funding for the Employment Service may be required, or the better use of existing funds. The decentralization of responsibility and the sharing of revenues under the Comprehensive Employment and Training Act are relevant here. The "new way" is simply to exercise executive authority that has been lying dormant too long.

# 3.
# "New Ways..." Continued

President Ford's 1974 address at the Ohio State commencement could easily have contained the following passage:

As societies become more complex in structure and resources, the need of formal or intentional teaching and learning increases. As formal teaching and training grow in extent, there is the danger of creating an undesirable split between the experience gained in more direct associations, and what is required in school. The danger was never greater than at the present time, on account of the rapid growth in the last few centuries of knowledge and technical modes of skills.

The man who actually said this was John Dewey,[1] writing near the turn of the century. To an educator like Dewey it was clear even then that intractable problems might arise in a rapidly developing technological society were the world of education to be isolated from the broader universe of experience.

Nevertheless, for what was to be most of another half century, the prevailing concern was to keep young people in school and to keep work from diverting them from their books:

* Compulsory school legislation was consciously designed to discourage parents from sending their children to work and to protect youth from the abuses of the workplace.
* Among some parents, additional education for their children—first high school, then college—became a symbol of their own status.
* Those who had worked hard from an early age to attain a

measure of success and security saw education as a more fruitful and pleasant path for their children to the same goals.

● School administrators preoccupied with their own institutions' growth and development paid little attention to the contributions of "outside" experiences to a youth's education.

● As years of schooling were extended, educational credentials became a substitute for work experience as the accepted means of qualifying for employment.

Yet all this was bound to change, and today agreement seems to be fast developing with respect to the forms the changes must take. They promise to affect the substance, even the structure of education, and to go to the basic nature and function of youth employment. The trend is most clearly seen in four particulars: first, in the increased consciousness that the whole pattern of "liberal arts" and "vocational" education must be woven together in a symbiotic rather than a separate, sometimes antagonistic, relationship; second, in the substantial agreement that some form of work or service experience must be included in, or interspersed with, the educational process; third, in the growing tendency to challenge the notion that all of the now greatly extended period of education should be taken—by all individuals—at one continuous sitting; fourth, in the enlarged public awareness of the need to review, modify, or repeal those customs, practices, laws, and institutionalism, adopted ostensibly for the protection of youth, that in fact operate to bar the effective interrelation of education and work and thus impede the transition from youth to adulthood.

Before examining these developments in detail, it is important— especially in connection with the first two—to recognize a distinction between elementary and secondary education on the one hand and postsecondary or "higher" education on the other. Although these emerging changes are important at all levels, they have already taken place to a larger extent at the college or university level. Change comes more easily in higher education, a fact noted in the opening sentence of Alden Dunham's report: "In a nutshell, the most salient characteristics of state colleges and regional universities are rapid change of function and astounding growth."[2]

The need for still further development in higher education has recently been the subject of comprehensive and penetrating study and analysis, notably by the Carnegie Commission on Higher Education under Clark Kerr's direction and by Frank Newman and his associates in their *Report on Higher Education*.[3] In this prospectus, principal emphasis is on the elementary and, even more, secondary school situation.

## INFUSION: CAREER EDUCATION

In 1971 the then U.S. Commissioner of Education, Sidney Marland, used a new phrase—"career education"—to identify a concept for infusing the entire process of elementary and secondary education with larger elements of career-oriented content. Deliberately and explicitly, he refrained from giving the phrase precise definition. Nor did he spell out what forms he thought this "infusion" should take, urging instead a variety of experimentation to determine what changes would be most effective.

The Marland proposal has evoked considerable controversy. Some have felt that it suggests more dilution of the ideal of a liberal arts education than is wise. Others have reacted to career education as being only a diversion of attention from the larger promise of vocational education, for which a broad and firm institutional base has already been established. The proposal sometimes attracts greater interest outside the educational establishment than within it. It has, nevertheless, had a strong, constructive catalytic effect. Surprisingly, it has had its greatest receptivity in the elementary schools, a significant percentage of which have made modifications. The going has been hardest in the secondary schools, a circumstance that most authorities are inclined to attribute to the rigidity that has developed there.

What was started by Commissioner Marland, through strong personal leadership and with very little money, promises to sink roots deep into the educational structure. Those efforts are now formalized by legislation in a new Office of Career Education, led by Kenneth Hoyt, whose efforts to date give every indication that the idea is still vital.

Success will, of course, depend as much on what transpires *outside* the classroom as within it and in this connection it is vital that the broader approach provide larger exposure for teachers—as well as students—to "work experience." How teachers prepare themselves, how they themselves relate to the nonacademic world, how they build the widest possible relevance into their materials and classroom approaches—indeed the very concept of teaching—all need to be reexamined. The potential for renewal through experience sabbaticals is ripe for exploration and evaluation. Obviously, the more teachers become involved in related but different out-of-school activities the more they want to do their in-school work in different ways, for different amounts of time, at different hours, and during different parts of the year.

Teaching need not, probably should not, be restricted to those for whom it is a full-time activity. A reporter who, a couple of months a year, spends the afternoon with students curious about the way a newspaper works, can introduce a dimension of immediacy and reality into the learning environment that is simply beyond the experience of a full-time teacher. In school systems where such arrangements exist, not only are regular teachers kept closer in touch with life outside the classroom, but the outsiders learn more about the realities of adolescence and education.

Programs such as these might, in the long run, have the effect of introducing into the curriculum needed new perspectives on work, of a sort to change those mindsets that have for so long made many jobs seem less desirable than they should be. That the schools could do more to change our attitudes about work is a monumental understatement. How many of us have been led, in our history courses, to the understanding that slavery has created a lasting prejudice against work once done by slaves? How many occupations—farm labor, domestic service, waiting tables, preparing food—have been victims of the American past? How many American high school students learn that in Paris waiters and cooks are respected for what they do? How many of us are aware that occupational status in America has been peculiarly complicated by the successive waves of new immigrants, ever taking the available jobs and leaving them tagged as less desirable, because they are the jobs of the new arrivals, those least accepted in the New World?

How long will parents urge white-collar work on their children, even when blue-collar work may be more challenging and financially more rewarding? Why is professional football a desirable job, when the opposing team is out to maim you physically, when you are expected to work even with a broken arm, and when keeping an edge on your opponent is to court permanent addiction to uppers and downers? To what extent could we increase the number of "good" jobs simply by changing our attitudes? To what extent are our groundless preferences shaped by what is taught or not taught in the schools?

The need to reassess what is being done—or not being done—today is particularly strong at the high school level. But the general infusion of "career" elements will not be achieved only by looking at those changes in schools identified directly with career education. *We need to start at the beginning, with the proposition that we no longer really know what is going on in American schools, and get on with the hard job of finding out.*

The most impressive case for "starting at the beginning" is set forth in the comprehensive examination of the history of the process of transition to adulthood in the United States, commissioned by the President's Science Advisory Committee and conducted by a panel chaired by James Coleman. The central conclusion from this study, published in 1973, is that youth are becoming increasingly isolated by schools both from adults and from life experiences.[4]

A particularly promising study is now going on under the auspices of the Institute for Development of Educational Activities (IDEA). Directed by John Goodlad, the project is titled simply "A Study of Schooling U.S.A." The size of the undertaking, begun in 1973, is illustrated by the target date for completion—1980. Its purpose according to the study description, is:

. . . first, to describe in detail the programs and processes characterizing a representative segment of elementary and secondary schooling in the United States; second, to compare this description with alternative models of exemplar schooling and, third, to provide a detailed agenda for systematic improvement of our precollegiate educational system.[5]

Unless we find out what is going on, and not going on, in the schools, we will remain vulnerable to such simplistic suggestions as that recently made by a governor to eliminate the twelfth grade altogether in his state.

This same need for "infusion" of the liberal arts and the vocational elements is felt at the higher education level, though in different form. The need there is for a larger diversity of curricula and emphases, so that young people with different interests and expectations can pursue different courses. The Newman *Report on Higher Education* inveighs strongly against too much homogeneity in higher education. Noting the virtual tripling of higher education enrollments in the past quarter century, George Tolley comments that "higher education, the world over, responded to the demand for more by offering more of the same."[6] At the same time, and with particular relevance to the interrelation of education and work, Howard Bowen and others have pointed out that the truest liberalization of education properly includes both diversifying the opportunities it affords and enlarging its relevance to the work and broader life experience—but without limiting education to meeting skill needs of the economy. The Carnegie Commission has developed this concept in detail in its reports on "Less Time More Options," "Diversity By Design," and "Toward a Learning Society."

In view of its full consideration elsewhere, the career element in higher education is not taken up further here, except with respect to one development of notable, and in a sense separate, significance. *One of the "new ways" the President calls for unquestionably involves the further development of community and junior colleges— not just in number and size but even more in the clearer establishment of their own distinct identity.*

Today some 3 million people attend such institutions, representing a sixfold enrollment increase in the past twenty years. Enrollments doubled during the 1960s, and projections indicate another doubling during the 1970s, with an expected 5 million students attending community and junior colleges by 1980.[7] Such enrollment increases, actual and projected, clearly suggest significant institutional vitality. But it is still hard to tell with any precision or certainty just what is happening, in part because community colleges are now identified as being part of the higher education or postsecondary education complex. Their particular and unique characteristics tend to get buried in the data and data categories designed essentially to monitor the progress and characteristics of colleges and universities. But an even more fundamental reason is that the institutions themselves are not clear yet about either their charter or their agenda for action.

They are obviously developing new sources of strength: their close ties to communities (in both physical proximity and spirit); their relative freedom from educational traditionalism and from the need to maintain established forms of quality; their open admissions and their low- or no-tuition policies, which make them particularly important to the equalizing of educational opportunity; and their extraordinarily varied educational clientele, consisting of adults (the average age of the community college student is twenty-seven), women, minorities, and the "disadvantaged," as well as substantial numbers of conventional postsecondary students.

These institutions, whose history actually goes back to the start of the century, were initially designed to correspond to the first two years of college or university. It was William Rainey Harper's view that they were needed to provide education at this level for people who either could not attend four-year colleges or were reluctant to do so. Throughout the 1950s and 1960s, community colleges acted principally as sifting or screening institutions for regular four-year colleges and universities. In some places the community colleges have come to be the prime providers of the first two years of "higher education," leaving it to the regular colleges and universities to tend to the educational needs of upper-division and graduate students. Indeed, there are some fifty upper-division universities in the United States today that depend almost solely upon the community colleges as feeder institutions.

But, as the enrollment boom has tapered off, and as community colleges have come to serve new clientele with special needs and interests, their programs have focused increasingly on occupational development. Today, only about 35 percent of community college students are in transfer programs, whereas 44 percent are in occupational programs that lead to an Associate of Arts degree but which have job entry as a main objective. In 1965 only 13 percent of community college students were in these latter programs.[8]

The central purpose of these colleges is gradually emerging as that of bringing together those resources necessary to meet the needs of people in the local community who are confronted with increasingly complex decisions about what to do next with their lives and where and how to go about doing it. As Edmund Gleazer, President of the American Association of Community and Junior Colleges, puts it: "In the phrase 'community college' the accent too often has been on the word 'college'"[9] and Alan Pifer: ". . . community colleges should start thinking about themselves from now on only secondarily as a sector of higher education and regard as their primary role community leadership."[10]

Given such a central charter, community colleges tend to feature transfer and occupational educational programs, as it is these programs that provide linkages to the sytems of higher education and employment on which their relevance depends. It would be wrong, however, to assess community colleges precisely in terms of how many enrolled in transfer programs go on to college (and what grades they get) or how many enrolled in occupational programs actually get jobs and at what salary level. If these are to be genuine community institutions, the necessary standard of judgment must be, "Are the people who come to the community colleges helped by whatever education, experience or guidance they receive there?" Take, for example, the person who, dissatisfied with his or her present place of employment, goes to the community college confused about what to do next. The individual enters a transfer program but after one year quits and goes to a proprietary school to specialize in some particular vocation. Or perhaps he or she decides to go back to the earlier employment. This person may well be a community college success story, to the degree that the guidance, education, and experience

51

provided, and the maturity gained there, contributed to some firmer personal choice and commitment.

The community college is currently far from being first and foremost a community institution. For it to be so, a new mix of personnel must be introduced and new links to the community established. Guidance and counseling services must be vastly expanded, and new means of assessing success devised. Critical issues, centering around problems of financing, accreditation, assessment, and faculty-union relations, impede developments in this direction. Many of these community colleges are still playing the game of trying to secure larger respectability within the higher education establishment—at the price of the inventiveness that is their license and their function. As Leland Medsker points out, the rhetoric of community involvement presently far outstrips its scope.[11] Nevertheless, this new order of community institutions is essential to making education a lifetime venture.

*It is imperative, then, that first priority be placed on infusing—in the truest sense—"liberal arts" and "vocational" education.* This is what the term "career education" implies and should be accepted as meaning. The reluctance so far to recognize this reflects the entrenchment of established bureaucracies more than any valid difference in principle.

## WORK OR SERVICE EXPERIENCE

The roots of vocational education reach far back into the history of American policy and legislation. When the Congress decided (in the Morrell Act of 1862) to subsidize colleges through land grants, it directed that these colleges be for training young people in the "agricultural and mechanical arts." There has been specific federal support for vocational education at the secondary school level ever since the Smith-Hughes Act of 1917.

It has, however, been only comparatively recently that any real effort has been made to tie general and vocational education significantly together. For most high school students, vocational training meant only the simplest exposures to "manual training" and "home economics." There was little suggestion or even notion of any kind of outside work experience. Some machinery and equipment from the workplace were put into two or three classrooms, usually in the high school basement. Sometimes a special curricular track was developed for a separate group of students. The work that some students did, either part-time while in school or during vacations, summers, and holidays, was in no way tied in with their schooling. School and work were, for the most part, still conceived of as unrelated, even conflicting, activities. There were exceptions to this, however, and they have accumulated at an increasing rate.

The first thought-out, formal attempt to *mix* education and work at the secondary school level was the adoption in Dayton, Ohio, in 1913, of the cooperative education program that had been developed a few years earlier at the University of Cincinnati for use at the higher education level. This was largely attributable to the encouragement of a prominent Dayton industrialist, John Patterson, who felt it imperative that educators and employers cooperate to provide youth with the skills necessary to qualify them for the workplace. Co-operative education developed in Dayton as a program of vocational education through a jointly planned and supervised arrangement between school and employers, alternating classroom study with on-the-job experience.

High school cooperative education programs were gradually adopted in a number of other cities, often without the benefit of outside financial support. These programs demonstrated a remark-able staying power, most of them surviving the Depression years. What evaluations were made of their effectiveness, from a variety of perspectives, were mostly favorable.

But it was not until the passage of the Vocational Education Act of 1963 that enrollments in secondary-level cooperative education programs went up dramatically. This Act substantially increased the total amount of federal money going to the support of vocational education and, for the first time, permitted use of this money to finance outside work experience. The Vocational Education Amendments of 1968 set aside separate funds for the expansion of cooperative vocational education, thus effectively serving to supplement the amount of money states were already using for this purpose from their own and other federal sources. Today almost half a million students are enrolled in cooperative programs funded with Federal Vocational Education monies.[12]

Cooperative education represents an effort to use actual work experience as a means of providing youth with specific occupational training while still in the education system. In many instances the provision of work opportunities also makes it possible economically for youth to continue in school. With the passage of the Vocational Education Act of 1963, specific funds were set aside for the support of work-study opportunities "as a source of income to needy students."

In 1972, 23,300 secondary school students were funded under this legislative provision.[13]

The Neighborhood Youth Corps In-School program, established in 1964, was also directed at providing income-generating work opportunities for those students wanting to stay in school but unable to do so without additional economic resources. In 1971 some 173,000 youth were provided part-time work opportunities under NYC In-School legislation.[14] In addition, a variety of other efforts were initiated to prevent premature school-leaving; many of these contained work experience components. For example, the Work Experience and Career Exploration Program (WECEP) is aimed at providing employment opportunities for fourteen- and fifteen-year-old youth as part of a program to make school more relevant for those inclined to leave it. Many other programs containing work experience and work exposure components are cooperatively arranged between local schools and employers as parts of a campaign to encourage youth to stay in school through graduation.

To judge from available information, which is seriously incomplete and unreliable, some 800,000 juniors and seniors in high school (13 percent of the total) are currently enrolled in arranged work experience programs. Less than half of these programs, however, are at all closely related to educational experience.[15]

Recently, educators and others have begun to turn their attention to using work experience as a means of serving objectives that go beyond specific occupational and skill training, income maintenance permitting continued educational attendance for the needy, and encouragement of students to stay in school longer. For example, the New York Board of Education and the city's Human Resources Administration have initiated an Executive High School Internship Program in which students (some 2000 in 1973-74) spend a semester with an official in government, education, or a variety of private agencies; keep a journal of their activities; and present a project to the school at the close of the semester. At the Skyline Center in Dallas students can participate in a career cluster as well as be involved in "out-of-center" situations.[16]

What formal evaluation there has been of the effectiveness of these various work experience initiatives has been on the whole encouraging, although the data have been so focused on particular program features that it is difficult to generalize from their findings.[17] What has emerged more clearly is the recognition that regard for this kind of learning in no way implies any devaluation of a good education in literature, mathematics, history, and so on. Quite the opposite. All the evidence suggests that education in the basic skills and humanities will be advanced, not retarded, by combining it with experience—that education comes from a chance to participate in society's pursuits as well as in a classroom. Again there is John Dewey's prescient counsel, that "the development within the young of attitudes and dispositions necessary to the continuous and progressive life of a society cannot take place by conveyance of beliefs, emotion and knowledge. It takes place through the intermediary of the environment."

*What is called for now is a synthesizing of these various forms of work experience: the traditional vocational education programs, the school-arranged work-study and cooperative education programs, and the extensive work that students are arranging for on their own.*

Further development is also desirable in a number of administrative arrangements and procedures. For instance:

The *year-round school,* which usually divides the school year into quarters, permits students to take holidays at times other than the conventional summer period. Accordingly, it expands the number of work opportunities for students on vacation and looking for seasonal work.

*Flexible modular scheduling* provides opportunities to shape educational programs to the needs of individuals. The hours of the school are arranged to permit unscheduled class time to be used for independent or individual study, volunteer service, or work experience.

*Revisions in average daily attendance regulations* permit the more flexible use of outside work experience opportunities that relate to the educational program. In Maryland students can now spend up to 50 percent of their day in outside work experience and still get full credit for daily school attendance.

*Credit for relevant work experience* is often granted now at both the secondary and higher education levels, with the amount of credit depending on the character of the work experience program. For example, in Syracuse, New York, students in the "Office Occupations Work Experience Program" receive one-half credit for each 300 hours on the job; students in the "Vocational-Industrial Cooperative Diversified Occupations Program" receive one credit for each 400 hours on the job.[18] In other experiments, among them the University Year for Action, and the High School Executive Internships program, students spend their full time away from the educational institution, with minimal reporting requirements, and are granted full academic credit for the period spent at work.

*External degree options* at both secondary and higher education levels also provide opportunities, directly or indirectly, for students to use work experience as a means of obtaining academic credit.

But beyond these administrative details, and underlying them, is the need for a clearer definition of the practical objectives sought and for a sound institutional base for accomplishing them. The most significant emergent—and practical—objective is to provide every high school age boy and girl with the opportunity for a significant work or service experience. It is reasonable, today, to set this objective in terms of at least 500 hours of such experience. This could be an *outside* work or service experience related directly to the education experience. But there are very real values in virtually any kind of work or service—sometimes the rougher (and more different from what the individual will later engage in) the better.

*Present experimentation with work experience alternatives should perhaps be directed toward developing a "community internship" as a standard, though not necessarily compulsory, element in secondary education.* Doubts are being increasingly voiced about whether either the circumstances or the nature of regular private employment alone will allow for the kind and amount of work experience contemplated here. What is envisaged is work or service experience that includes all the disciplines of the competitive arena. It probably ought to be work, or service, for pay, although there is considerable and respectable disagreement about this matter.

Such community internships would contribute significantly to the purpose reflected in the increasingly widespread suggestion that there be more emphasis on citizenship education at the secondary and postsecondary levels. Civics courses aren't enough. A Special Committee of the American Bar Associaton is now giving particular attention to the desirability of including in the elementary and secondary curricula, materials exposing children to the basic idea that a democracy's functioning depends on people's realization that its strength comes only from their participation in the exercise of these functions. But here again, doing is the best form of learning. The argument is at least as strong for government experience as for work experience in young people's training for their future prospects and responsibilities.

A procedure and system for administering such programs, including the enlistment and organization of the wider community resources, will be suggested in Chapter 4.

Present economic circumstances suggests particularly the necessity to deal with the impact of the business cycle on the youth preparation period. If experience is to be brought within the preparation period of life and recognized as an important part of the process of education, the arrangements for it must not only be solid enough to withstand the shifts that afflict the economy but relate to these shifts in a sensible way.

An economy like that of 1968 and 1969 made many more things possible, including a reasonably phased enlargement of work experience programs. Today, it is more likely to be asked why the nation should concern itself with workplace experience for young people when millions of adults are out of work. In the vocabulary of the past, when "education" was for youth, and "work" for adults, why indeed? The answer changes, must change, when experience is itself recognized as education. If there was ever a time when public *education* for youth was curtailed because the GNP took one of its periodic dips, it is too long ago to be remembered. Experience must be admitted to that same protected environment.

What this means is that factory floors, retail trade counters, and finance counting tables must be used as extensions of the classroom, and that such use be accepted by employers, workers, and union leaders. What it *must not* mean is the displacement of adults from their regular jobs during recession periods *as a result* of the use of student labor. A whole set of rules and practices will have to evolve to accomplish this result, along such lines as these:

• Creating new roles—helping adults produce, for instance, as distinguished from holding regular jobs.
• An increase in use of employer facilities during nonproduction hours (such as hiring regular employees as "instructors") as a close approximation of the adult work situation. A recognition of employer costs is probably necessary here, but tempered by what will often be recognized by the employer as a preferred means of preparing his own future labor supply.
• An increase in unpaid public service experience opportunities—a greater reliance, for example, on "community internships" to provide the experience settings.
• Enlargement of public programs such as the Neighborhood Youth Corps.* The creation of public service jobs for students from poor families is especially critical in times of high unemployment.

---

*While new federal manpower legislation has eliminated this title, such efforts are authorized at the discretion of local communities.

57

Youth

More than the development of any "program" approach to the problem is the necessity to start thinking of the workplace and the community as a place where, in part, youth get educated. The education budget must shoulder its appropriate share of the costs. This means, to be sure, that the education budget must go up and down with the business cycle, a prospect not unwelcome from the standpoint of national economic management. Yet American enterprise may be expected to recognize the validity of maintaining experience opportunities during recession periods. It may further be expected to recognize a longer-term economic reward in a better prepared, more responsible, youth labor force—as long as the public sector fully meets its responsibilities.

Here again, as in the preceding section, particular emphasis has been deliberately placed on the need for development of larger work or service experience opportunities at the secondary school level. There is another whole story of the development of "cooperative education" at the postsecondary level. But this need has been much more fully recognized and met there—at Antioch College, Northeastern University, Beloit College, at increasing numbers of what have been traditionally liberal arts institutions, and now particularly in the community and junior colleges. There is no point in repeating this story here. It is among the sixteen-to-eighteen-year-old group, those at upper high school levels, that there is today the largest need for further development of this kind of opportunity.

## A CONSIDERED BREAK

*The now almost certain next major step in "fusing" the education and work experiences is to provide much more extensive opportunity—where individual circumstances warrant it—for a student's stepping out of the educational sequence for a year or two and then coming back into it.* A great deal of this is already being done, with, so far as we know, almost uniformly beneficial effect.

The proposition would not be advanced if the stepping out is into nothing. The value lies in what would be a "considered break." The structures we build for counseling and guidance would need to help youth choose when best to do it, as well as what to do.

This is another instance where the education establishment cannot do the job by itself. The impetus, however, can begin there, riding on what may be a wave of student interest, even practice, that in many instances may be in front of any existing attempts to legitimize such a procedure.

58

At least some of the things that qualify for a "considered break" are community service work and paid employment. But with more experience, and careful consideration, it may be possible to open up new opportunities for constructive use of such breaks. In Canada a system has been introduced under which young people design their own work or service programs, present them to the schools for approval, and then receive a stipend for carrying them out. In California a state Commission for the Reform of Intermediate and Secondary Education has recently recommended a "furlough" system under which students would receive education credit for various kinds óf work, professional service, or travel experience, with the school acting as the "broker" for such arrangements.[19]

There are both formal and informal barriers to a break in schooling that need to be removed. Basic Educational Opportunity Grants now exclude people who started college before April 1, 1973, and want to reenter. A great many colleges still look with disfavor on students who leave and then want to return.

There is the richness that may be found in experience. There is the maturity that seems to come from doing. There is the possibility of greater access to college from student earning, when the pressure for going straight through is removed. And there is at least the possibility of a better-informed choice as to what kind of education ought to be sought when the time comes to step back in.

The key to this door is to be found in a new procedure that recognizes that taking a "considered break" of this kind involves more than the individual youth and some one educational institution. It truly involves not only that individual but very often two different educational institutions (the one he or she leaves and the one later returned to), the employment or service communities, and the community at large. Here again, a proposal for meeting this procedural need will be made in Chapter 4.

### REMOVING BARRIERS

*The search for "new ways" of linking education and work must take account of the barriers to this evolution that are embodied in both law and custom relating to youth employment.*

Both federal and state laws entirely prohibit the employment during school hours of children under sixteen. Enacted many years ago to counteract a then widespread exploitive practice, these laws operate today to deny some forms of work experience that would be generally recognized as valuable. The problem here is not, however, a broad one, and a significant program has already been undertaken jointly by federal and state authorities to grant exceptions to these statutory provisions.[20] Surveys made by the Department of Labor indicate that work experience results in (or is at least accompanied by) substantial reductions in dropouts, truancy, and tardiness, as well as in significant improvements in school grades.[21] The findings appear sufficient to recommend amendment of the federal and state laws.

Federal and state prohibitions on persons under eighteen working in "hazardous occupations" are perhaps more significantly involved. Although the federal offices report that only about 5 percent of all employment is foreclosed to sixteen-and seventeen-year-olds by such prohibitions, employers manifest a considerable concern about their scope and a consequent reluctance to hire anybody under eighteen for fear of violating either federal or state laws.[22] It adds to this confusion that the types of employment alowed for fourteen- and fifteen-year-olds are considerably more limited than those allowed sixteen- and seventeen-year-olds.[23] A comprehensive effort must be made to eliminate these misunderstandings.

Though the hard evidence is lacking, it is widely conjectured that the minimum wage law contributes seriously to youth unemployment. Although a large-scale BLS investigation disclosed no conclusive evidence of significant effects of the minimum wage laws on the teenage employment situation,[24] there is unquestionably some level of statutory wage minimum that would adversely affect teenage employment. There is simply no evidence to establish what the level is.

The public debate on these subjects is emotional, stemming both from memories of Depression years and from subconscious legacies from earlier stages of the Industrial Revolution. If we are ever to get an objective view, we need to bring together the most factual information possible. We need a complete inventory of the extent and effect of laws, practices, and customs that needlessly constrain people's mobility between education and work at all stages of life. Most particularly, we need continuing analysis of the effect on the youth employment situation of such statutory measures as minimum wage laws, child labor laws, school attendance regulations, and prohibitions against youth working in hazardous occupations.

The most difficult but probably the most important part of this inventory will be not of the laws but of the employment practices that constrain education-work mobility. Is there, in fact, a developing practice of hiring male youths under twenty for only "youth-type" jobs, and of unnecessarily restricting entrance to "adult-type" jobs to college graduates, or perhaps to those with two years of postsecondary education? How much do the traditions of five eight-hour work days per week and of a preference for full-time, as against part-time, employment affect the intermixing of education and work? Are there hidden constraints on this type of mobility in typical seniority and pension plans in collective bargaining agreements?

The whole "credentialing" practice would properly be included here, as it affects entry and advance into and through both educational and employment levels.

The expansion of arranged work experience programs requires adaptations in the practices not only of educational institutions but of employing institutions. No less than the schools, business corporations have been slow to adapt their practices to meet work experience needs. Yet the success of cooperative education reflects an ultimate flexibility. So does the adjustment by employers to the problems arising under various federal manpower training programs.

In regard to this prospect, there is reason to take particular note of what is currently happening at the postsecondary educational level. During the eighteen months that this Prospectus has been in preparation, there has been a series of related developments. There have been *shrinking* enrollments in a great many four-year colleges and universities, particularly among those that have traditionally placed primary emphasis on a "liberal" education—and especially among the private (and usually higher tuition) colleges. A marked shift has occurred in student interest and enrollment from the humanities to the science courses. Applications for admission to graduate study, particularly in law, medicine, and engineering, have gone way up.

Now, however, college graduates and the holders of advanced degrees confront a new set of developments in the job market. The situation is that with national unemployment at the 9 percent level, layoff lists are so long that the prospect of any young person's finding a job—college degree or not—has been sharply reduced except in a few relatively specialized fields. There is a whole new questioning today of the relationship of college education to work, both in general and with particular application to the very large education industry itself.

This Prospectus simply cannot deal adequately with this set of developments. Many of them are new, although they could have been more fully anticipated. They derive in part from current economic

61

circumstance that still cannot be evaluated for intensity or duration.*

Preliminary consideration, however, has led to the recognition that this situation—involving more and more young people preparing themselves more and more fully for particular types of careers, only in some cases to find their career passage blocked perhaps even more by virtue of this preparation—highlights now the most significant "barrier" of all to interrelating education and work. There is simply no effective institutional structure or process, at either the federal or the state level, for achieving this organic relationship.

Combining government departments has been proposed too often for it to be considered a "new way." The National Manpower Institute Council members would, as individuals, be virtually unanimous in their endorsement of the 1972 proposal to establish a new federal Department of Human Resources. But that proposal got nowhere. The practical approach is apparently to press further along the lines of closer cooperation and coordination within the traditional structure.

Manpower needs and career outlook projections. . . . counseling and guidance and youth job placement . . . career education, work experience, break arrangements, and a more general approach . . . breaking down old barriers—what is "new" about any and all of these, so far as the *programs* are concerned, is only in drawing ther development.

If we are clearer now than we could have been ten years ago about programs and policies, this leaves the critical question of what *processes* will better put these programs and policies to work.

If these are the new ways, what are the new means?

---

*For a thorough treatment of the larger matter, see Margaret Gordon, ed., *Higher Education and the Labor Market* (Carnegie Commission on Higher Education, McGraw-Hill, 1974).

# 4.
# New Means

Only the community, acting as a committee of the whole, can provide the new means necessary to make the new ways effective. For the causes of the problems at the school-to-work passage reach far into the areas on both sides of it, beyond the competence of the education or work sovereignties to handle alone.

The difficulties a particular young person encounters at this exchange point are as likely to have their taproots in personal circumstance, of self and family, as in anything that either happens or doesn't happen between the ages of sixteen and twenty-one. But what is more relevant is that the problems faced by youth as a whole find only their most immediately proximate causes in what has happened to education and work. Important as these causes are—and the object of necessary attention—they must be considered in their critical context of a speeding and often reckless technology, a tightening bind between the earth's natural resources and its population, a psychologically deceptive affluence, and a frustrated revolution of rising expectations. It must be recognized further that a good many of these problems derive at least as much from what has happened to the institution of the family as from anything happening in the education and employment processes. The truth is, no other institution has emerged to do for maturing young people what the family used to do.

We and they are left, therefore, to deal with a disconcerting truth: Existing institutions, with their conflicting responsibilities and allegiances, simply do not see themselves as young people's agents vis-à-vis the adult world. The conventions of education and employment have to be changed, but these two sovereignties are unlikely to be effective partners in any fundamental corrective venture except as some new force is brought to bear.

The education and employment establishments are typical bureaucracies, essentially inertial. Between them is a long history of separatism, to the extent that one is considered "public," the other "private." They meet at a comparatively narrow frontier. Their primary orientations rarely connect with the needs that young people coming of age feel the most acutely: gaining insight into one's changing self; observing, experiencing, and evaluating adult roles; obtaining not only the specific skills prerequisite to employment but also those broader social, political, judgmental, and communication skills required for choosing, changing, or advancing within an adult environment.

Historically, the schools have been oriented toward improving cognitive skills, surveying the ideals of civilization and culture, developing an individual's sense of rationality and objectivity and appreciation for learning. They will move slowly to enlarge their objectives—especially as they are encouraged to stay put by the prevalent employer view: "If the schools will just send us young people who can read and write and add and think, we will hire them—and do the job training ourselves."

The primary business of business is still business, and the currency of "corporate social conscience" is inflated, except as it is based on the more classical corporate self-interest. There is further serious question about the effectiveness of what employers *can* do, at least so long as they are asked only to be cooperators in whatever the schools devise in the work-study and cooperative and career education areas.

Educators and employers must, to be sure—both as a matter of advancing their particular interests and discharging their responsibilities, and equally as a matter of institutional development—be the primary architects and builders of a more rational interrelationship between education and work. There must nevertheless be developed and exerted here a new force drawn from the broader community. The critical question in this whole policy area is whether the real community is now ready to stand up—not just to be counted, but also to take a large part again in handling its own affairs.

This reenlistment of the broader community will require thoughtful analysis and careful, persistent effort to accomplish something that isn't going to just happen. A model for such effort is developing today in Detroit, through the efforts of the Detroit Education Task Force.[1] A concept of tripartitism must be explored for better functioning of the community relationship; although it parallels roughly the concept that has evolved in labor-management relations, the prospect here is for the development of the public not as chairman but as itself a participating party of interest.

What would inevitably be left vague if expressed only as a concept can be better suggested in the form of a specific proposal: *that there be established at the local level what will be called here Community Education-Work Councils.*

Advisedly, at the present stage, the proposal is to do this on a pilot-project basis in twenty to twenty-five representative metropolitan and rural areas over a five-year period. An integral part of the proposal is that it include provision for an independent, tough-minded process for critical *evaluation,* to be initiated when the project is started and carried on through to cover every element of failure as well as success.

Purposes and functions of such Community Education-Work Councils are appropriately suggested first in broad terms, the details then to be added. Relying essentially on local community initiative, the Councils would ferry people and ideas across the gap between education and employment and at the same time infuse the coming-of-age process with knowledge and experience available from the broader community. They would facilitate the transition of the younger members of the community between institutionalized education and whatever is to follow it, although without commitment to the one-way order of experience this suggests. This function would include both the rendering of services directly to youth and the "brokering" of functions of established institutions—particularly schools, employing enterprises, labor unions, employment agencies, and families.

This proposal draws on more than considerations of education-work policy development alone. Preparing youth for adulthood used to provide part of the essential cement for community cohesion, cooperation, and identity. It still could. The realization grows that we have made a mistake in disengaging ourselves so completely from so many of our responsibilities, relying on representation as a substitute for participation.

There is today a manifest desire among more and more people, coping with a society suddenly grown vast, to find some way to participate effectively again in community affairs. People are tired of the feeling of shrinking just a little bit each day from nonuse. The easiest part of setting up a Community Education-Work Council would be the enlistment of qualified volunteers.

But the case for something of this nature—of a new institution that would take the transition from youth to adulthood, from education to work, as its particular responsibility—will ultimately depend more on experience than on logic. The record of effective social change is that at some point the emphasis has to be shifted from policy to process. An idea can be carried only so far on paper. Then it has to be put in the hands of stewards and managers who will test it out, who will try to make it work, who will find out whether it is going to fly or fall and what modifications it needs.

These Community Education-Work Councils would be composed of those people—as individuals and as representatives of institutions—who are in the best position to influence success at this critical passage. Who those people are thought to be will vary from community to community. There are, however, some obvious candidates in every community:

> Teachers and school administrators
> Employers
> Representatives of organized labor
> Representatives of manpower agencies
> Parents
> Civic leaders
> Students

The convening of such institutional representatives and individuals would, inevitably, introduce a larger prospect for rationality at the passage from education to employment. More, it would provide the means for cooperation in creating a sense of community.

In the beginning, a Council's working agenda would very possibly be drawn up from the program needs identified in Chapters 2 and 3, although, importantly, in an order reflecting the community's own sense of priority.

### COUNSELING - ADVICE

• As long as school counselor certification remains restricted, it would be a Council role to provide people from a variety of life backgrounds to talk to students about career plans and job problems—probably leaving the "guidance" to the professional counselors.

• The Council would institute a follow-up system for counseling and guidance activities and attempt to get such a system established within the schools.

• The Council would provide parents with career and vocational information to help them help their children.

Should the Council get directly, into the guidance and counseling business, through its own staff? Into job referrals and placements? Are the Council's services to be, in general, adjunctive or independent? What, more broadly, would be the relationship between this new kind of community agency and others already established?

So far as the guidance and counseling function is concerned, it is by nature so closely related to the work of the schools that there is good reason for institutionalizing it in the schools, where it would be easily accessible to most of the prospective beneficiaries of its services. An agency like a Community Education-Work Council would in effect act as (1) a kind of pressure group, insisting that the counseling function be discharged more fully, and (2) a supportive agency, supplying services needed to enhance and complement those of the counselors.

The Council could help infuse the counseling process with a larger understanding of what the "world of work" means in the particular community. People with other than academic experience could be obtained, through the Council's membership, from corporations and service agencies. There would be the opportunity, too, to help teachers incorporate occupational and career information into their courses. Where this is done through work-site visitations, the Council could perform a brokerage function, increasing the effectiveness of such programs and at the same time minimizing the demands on employers that develop when such arrangements are made in uncoordinated fashion by individual teachers.

The Councils would be in a superior position to work out procedures for involving in the counseling and guidance process those who are the most concerned: parents and young men and women. A Council might, for example, arrange a series of evening seminars to help parents better understand how younger people see themselves in relation to work and service.

Numerous surveys have disclosed that young people make their career decisions largely on the basis of information and misinformation they get within their peer groups. A Council could try to work out better forms of "rap sessions." It might also find ways to make available to young people the knowledge, experience, and perspective of those already employed, particularly those of younger employees.

Part of the Council's function would be to inventory the guidance services potentially available in the community and to promote their use. For the lack of such an inventory, many community resources go either untapped or underdeveloped.

It is hard to imagine a high school counselor's not wanting to make full use of such a community resource. If, however, the Council's proffers evoked insufficient response, it would consider establishing a counseling service of its own.

### OCCUPATIONAL INFORMATION

The development of a local occupational information system would be an important Council responsibility. This would include drawing on existing resources, such as those of the local manpower agency, and packaging the information in forms accessible to students.

A comprehensive Local Opportunity Inventory would include all work, service, and special training opportunities available to the community's youth. Private employers would supply such a Council with data about job openings and prospects that they are usually hesitant to give the Bureau of Labor Statistics and simply do not give the Employment Service. This information could be pooled, as it is virtually nowhere today, with parallel information on the public employment service opportunities. Local training programs, public and private, would be included. The Department of Labor's Manpower Administration has set up a new Office of Occupational Information to develop new systems and techniques for the distribution of available data, giving local communities a new resource to draw on.

The preparation and maintenance of an adequate Local Opportunity Inventory would be a large-scale undertaking, drawing necessarily on information from private and government employers, state and local education agencies, the Federal-State Employment Service, and the Bureau of Labor Statistics. Methods would have to be devised for translating national aggregate data into local terms and for putting the Bureau of Labor Statistics *Handbook* and *Guide* into more easily usable forms. The Councils might well become the first effective pressure groups demanding useful *local* information, influencing both the direction and scale of federal occupational outlook data.

Preparing, developing, and maintaining such an Inventory would require, in a medium-size community, two, or possibly three, professionally trained full-time staff members. The considerable paraprofessional assistance that would be required is readily available from volunteers—for one example, retired corporate personnel officers. The part-time use of women who are planning to turn to other occupations when their children get a little older would be a recognition of another transition between different life functions that these Councils might well have on their agenda. There would also be the doubly profitable possibility of identifying elements in setting up and maintaining this Inventory that would provide the substance for a high school or college seminar, or for the employment of several interns in off-campus work study.

It is a harder job, more of an art, to make projections of future job prospects. Councils would be encouraged in such an effort, however, by what has been done in the Manpower Management Information Dissemination Project in Ventura, California. Under the joint sponsorship of the public schools and the Ventura Community College, a continuing survey is made of local employers to determine present manpower needs and to project these needs through 1980. Students in the area are then asked to identify their areas of occupational interest and are grouped for counseling according to commonality of interest.

### PLACEMENT

What such Councils will find it possible to do to place young people in jobs will vary from community to community. But among other activities, they could be expected to:

• Apply for and obtain federal funds for school placement services as provided by the Education Amendments of 1972.

• Press for an adequate share of resources from the manpower agencies working with the agency responsible for local implementation of the Comprehensive Employment and Training Act.

• Attempt to get cooperative job placement services established in or near schools, working with the Employment Service, the CETA manpower agency, local and state school officers, and local employers. In some communities Council staff would probably function only as stimulators; other Councils might find it advisable to become operational.

• Follow up on youth after job placement, in cooperation with the local counselors.

• Promote relaxation of rigid age standards and give local employers whatever objective information is available about youth job performance.

The Councils would probably make efforts to "broker" partnerships between the schools and the Employment Service. Arrangements could be made for locating placement personnel in the schools. Beyond this, some Councils would consider the applicability in their particular localities of the broader kind of system established in Sweden, where the placement function is a joint enterprise of the Board of Education and the Labor Market Board, with management and financing shared equally.

## CAREER EDUCATION AND EDUCATION-EXPERIENCE

An Education-Work Council would provide an invaluable community base for the advancement of the kind of initiative that currently finds it fullest development in the career education concept. Looking, in effect, for that common ground which includes *both* liberal arts and vocational education, Commissioner Marland found himself—after making this proposal in 1971—with fewer allies on either side than might have been expected. Yet that proposal related closely to contemporary thinking in the general community about elementary and secondary education.

Such Councils would be in a superior position not just to administer but even more significantly to *develop* effective education-experience programs. If the planning for such programs *started* with the Councils, where employers would participate as full partners instead of often reluctant cooperators in school initiated enterprises, they would have a firm base, established in terms of *both* educational and employment interests. Then, as these programs might be broadened out to embrace even more significant community internship or work or service apprenticeship concepts, the necessary administrators of such broader programs would be engaged as architects as well.

Perhaps the initial Council function in this area would be simply to provide an efficient brokerage of work-study and cooperative education arrangements, thereby ending the confusion that results when each school approaches the employing establishment independently.

As part of a Council clearinghouse function, better arrangements could be worked out for the schools to monitor the work experience and to negotiate with employers on behalf of youth to improve the potential of work as a learning experience. Employers would have the opportunity to communicate their needs to the schools more fully and to observe correctable educational deficiencies. Indeed a major benefit of such a dovetailing would be the establishment of a firmer basis for informed and constructive criticism and advocacy of both the educational and employment systems. Differences would become clearer, convergent goals better understood. Schools could be expected to resist any weakening of education's broader purposes to accommodate employer demands for narrow skill training; employers could be counted on to correct any disregard by educators of the practical demands of employment.

It would be expected that the Councils would move beyond a concern with the day-to-day administration of work-study programs and on to broader related questions. Would there, for example, be improved opportunity for various kinds of experiential learning—and would youth job placement be easier—if high school calendars were put on a year-round basis, with arrangements permitting graduation at various times during the year instead of only in June?* What are the implications—for education, training, and work-study programs—of the changes going on in the nature of work, especially work done by persons under twenty?

Community Education-Work Councils would provide perhaps crucially important forums for working out—in terms of specific situations—answers to some problems affecting education-experience interchange that seem to defy solution when posed in broader conceptual terms. These involve, particularly, statutory provisions and common practices that restrict—or are commonly thought to restrict—youth employment and experiential learning programs: child labor laws, health and safety statutes and regulations, occupational licensing requirements, school attendance laws, minimum wage laws, collective bargaining contract provisions, and employer youth hiring practices.

In working up a Local Youth Opportunity Inventory, a Council could appropriately make a comprehensive survey of what jobs in the particular community are foreclosed to youth of different ages by these various laws and regulations. Where in particular instances technological change or the revision of work processes was found to have made the existing laws or regulations anachronistic, the Council could initiate action necessary to revise them.

Given an institution for such local review and informational programs and the now reasonably hoped-for willingness of federal and state authorities to allow modifications, existing child labor and school attendance laws would appear to present no obstacles to the establishment of the types of programs being proposed here. The

---

*This has been the conclusion in Dallas.

harder questions are about the effect on such programs of various statutes and practices relating to compensation.

Discussion in this area invariably centers on the endless dispute about whether youth employment should—and would—be stimulated by including a "youth differential" in the minimum wage laws. The argument is fruitless, pursued in terms of national legislative policy, for adversary positions are now polarized beyond any practical possibility of accommodation. Yet the questions involved seem entirely open to rational resolution at the local community level, in the context of particular situations.

A Council, for instance, could consider the remuneration issue in terms of the proper and necessary context of what is essentially a youth transition program, with full account taken of all services rendered and all values received. The answers are not limited to "no compensation" or "full wages" or a "fixed differential." There are such other possibilities as public subsidies (characteristic of education), subsistence payments (in the Peace Corps pattern), training stipends (as in various manpower training programs)—and combinations of these. If the individuals involved are thought of not just as students or employees but as interns or apprentices, different sets of remunerative practices offer relevant analogies.

A particular Council would probably work out a variety of transitional programs, with due consideration being given to whatever compensatory arrangements would be appropriate under the different circumstances. Where younger age groups are involved, the work experience might consist of no more than a series of orientation or exposure sequences, where the question of pay wouldn't even come up. At the other extreme, in situations involving upper teenagers holding down entry or near-entry jobs and alternating periods of work and periods of school, wages clearly should be paid at statutory levels. With respect to arrangements coming between these extremes, a Council—including representatives of all the interests involved— would take into account the degree to which the work or the education element is predominant at a particular stage of development, the comparative values involved and received, the employment abilities of different groups of youth, and the reality of local job conditions.

There is ample basis for reasonable confidence that arrangements of this kind could be worked out by a Council in complete consistency with the minimum wage laws, giving full regard to organized labor's legitimate concern about youth differentials becoming exploitive conveniences and to the equally legitimate objection of employers to being asked to subsidize these transitional programs.

The question of educational "credit" for work-study and other experiential learning programs is in a sense the other side of the "compensation" coin. The two items could be placed together on a Community Council agenda—if only for the purpose of advising the school authorities of community reactions to what is obviously a matter lying within the schools' particular jurisdiction.

There is, furthermore, a clear and important commonality of interest about the scheduling of both academic and work-experience offerings to facilitate collaborative arrangements. Almost all American secondary education is scheduled on a 9 a.m. to 3 p.m. basis, with five-day-a-week attendance required. More flexibility will be needed if more work experience is to be built into the formal educational programs. Employers, for their part, will differ about how part-time student help can be fitted into production and service schedules—on a split-day, one-day-a-week, weekends-only, alternate-week, or some other basis. There is an obvious brokerage function here for Councils.

Similarly, but with even larger significance, there is a potential Council function in connection with the development of a "considered break" option as part of the recognized formal secondary and postsecondary education pattern. If an individual is giving responsible consideration to going "out" for a year or two and then back "in," a full and perhaps continuing consideration of this plan, with the kind of staff a Community Education-Work Council could provide, would be obviously invaluable. It should perhaps even be prescribed as a condition of such a break.

It seems no exaggeration to suggest, in general, that whatever validity there is—and it appears to be a great deal—in the idea of building an experience element into the formal educational sequence, this idea depends for its viability on the development of some such institution as a Community Education-Work Council.

## EDUCATIONAL INTERCHANGES

Community Education-Work Councils might also provide the catalyst for the now long-overdue closer coordination of various different kinds of institutionalized educational offerings and opportunities.

Just as there should be more flexible arrangements for alternating education and experience, there should be arrangements, too, for giving young people the opportunity to "mix" their general education with more vocationally oriented training. This is already happening where—as is true now in many cities—technical high schools are being added to the public school systems, with provision for individual students to spend time in both. But this is by no means the general situation.

Various other new efforts are being made to interrelate general and vocational public education. But in too many places this remains a virtual arms-length relationship between separate institutional bureaucracies. A Community Council, interesting itself in this often absurd situation, could be a highly effective force for efficiency, economy, and enriched student opportunity.

Obvious opportunities also exist for closer working relationships between high school systems and postsecondary institutions such as technical institutes and community colleges. There is every reason for some students to begin some parts of their postsecondary education before completing their high school work. It all depends on the interest and competence of the student and the opportunities available in the community. This is well recognized: in 1972 the College Entrance Examination Board gave advanced placement examinations to 59,000 high school students who had already completed college-level courses.[2] Here again a Community Council could have a significant influence on extending this kind of opportunity to young people who are not going on to get baccalaureate degrees.

Such a Council might also be able to do what so far remains almost entirely neglected with respect to private, or proprietary, technical and vocational schools. At last count, there were more than 7000 of these schools in the country.[3] They are by no means all good schools; some are very bad, and a lot of them are guilty of unconscionable false advertising. Still, a lot of young people are using these schools, and some of them have undeniably good track records. It is foolish to treat them, as a matter of public policy, as though they don't exist.

A Community Education-Work Council could properly and profitably go into this private proprietary school situation: to distinguish those that are responsible from those that are not in a local community, to find out more about the elements of the unquestionable success some of them have had in handling situations and cases the public schools have had trouble with, and even to consider whether there are possibilities for mutually advantageous collaborative arrangements as the need for more experiential learning becomes increasingly recognized.

74

The position of public secondary schools would be advantaged, not diminished, by attention to these possibilities. Left to pursue more traditional educational objectives, they would be less vulnerable to charges of inattention to areas in which public insistence has overextended them.

It remains to recognize the questions that inhere in any suggestion for setting up a new institution. Who does it? How is it financed? What is its authority? What is its relationship to the established institutions? Won't this be just one more "committee" when there are already too many? Where will it get its staying power when the novelty of it wears off? Wouldn't it be better to try to work within the present school and governmental systems?

So far as the specifics are concerned, the proposal is simply that this be *tried* in twenty to twenty-five communities on a five-year basis. The proposal is advanced here only after confirmation from experience that there is a growing desire in communities to do something about matters that have been neglected or left solely to public government.

The costs involved are between $100,000 and $250,000 per year per community. Already authorized and appropriated federal funds—in several different departmental budgets—could be put to this purpose. But this project should not be dependent entirely on federal financing. There has been a clearly manifested private foundation interest in such a project. *Local* participation in the financing of such Councils should be sufficient to meet any question about where complete control of them lies. Unless this can be developed as a *community* project—in every respect—there is no point in doing it.

And only in the trying of it will some of the more specific questions about how, or whether, it works be answered. From time to time we will need to relax the traditional rules of rationality if we are to come up with new ways to deal with social policy. Western civilization suffers at this point from a rationalist bias that assumes that all activity follows purpose. In reality, human beings frequently discover purpose in the course of experiencing activity. A Community Council would provide the context of responsibility within which experimental venture could be most boldly undertaken.

The proposal rests, more fundamentally, on the conviction that enough people want very much today to reestablish their role in the handling of their own affairs, that this can be done most meaningfully at the local level, and that the closer tying in of youths' education and what comes after it is a good assignment to start on.

The suggested form of citizen involvement is not advanced as a challenge to the established educational and employment institutions. On the contrary. Educational and corporate and labor union representatives would be among the principal architects of such Councils, and whatever may be accomplished along the suggested lines will properly and inevitably be done through established organizations. The point is rather that without the assumption by the wider community of some of the responsibilities involved, the efforts of enlightened leadership within the narrower school and employment communities will be inevitably ineffective. It would be unrealistic to suggest that the establishment of these new instruments of community will be easy. It won't be. Inevitable tensions will develop between such Councils and institutions already in place. But productive tension is probably an essential element in constructive change. Existing institutions become function-oriented; their original purposes get pushed back by the pressures of the regularities by which they maintain their daily existence. Productive tension must come in large part from outside. One of the proper concerns here will be to see that such Councils do not become so busy justifying themselves that this purpose of change is too timidly served.

Perhaps it won't work at all. There is, though, Antigone's counsel: "Until we have *tried* and failed, we haven't failed." This seems, in short, worth trying.

# II: The Career Years

Eight years ago Jack Fuller of Akron, Ohio was selling graduation accessories (caps and gowns and fraternity pins). He was spending an average of four nights a week on the road "going like the hammers of hell," had picked up 30 extra pounds of flab and complained of a nervous stomach. He was making more than $30,000 a year.

On their 16th wedding anniversary Fuller and his wife Lee (short for Lenore) opened a bottle of champagne. "All of a sudden," says Fuller, "we realized that we'd been married 16 years and never done any of the things we'd meant to do. I had always wanted to go to Alaska, and Lee wanted just as badly to go to the Virgin Islands. So we said let's do something before it's too late." Years before, Fuller had been a high school football coach, and Lee had a teaching certificate. It occurred to him that he and Lee still had a chance to live out their plans: they could become teachers, first in Alaska for two years, and then in the Virgin Islands.

Before that evening the Fullers had never thought seriously about leaving Akron; afterward they could think of nothing else. Jack wrote to the Bureau of Indian Affairs asking for any position above the Arctic Circle. He enrolled at Akron University for his teaching certificate. Eventually the BIA found them teaching jobs in an Arctic whaling village called Point Hope. And a year and a half after that bottle of champagne, ignoring the cries of their friends ("We have a new tennis club and a new swimming pool, and you're leaving?"), the Fullers rented their colonial house, stored their furniture and took off.

"Beginning Again in the Middle" by Ann Bayer, *Life,* June 12, 1972.

"I really do believe that work is the most important thing in your life. It keeps you going. It keeps you alive, actively interested, it keeps the juices flowing. I have a horror of being dependent on my children. I think women are more and more finding out they've got to do something, not to compete with men, but to have something for themselves. Everything works better when you're working.

"I've worked all my life and I have nothing to my name but my apartment at the Dakota in New York City.... I have a child to support and after each job I think, Christ, will I ever work again. . . . I'm unemployed now and they make it really tough to collect unemployment, and I've earned it. You have to stand in line for hours and answer a lot of questions. I haven't done it yet, but I should."

> Lauren Bacall, actress, quoted by Sally Quinn, *The Washington Post,* January 21, 1975.

The 41-year-old Manhattan housewife had spent 20 years doing volunteer work for churches, hospitals, and schools. And then when she got home, she had a husband and six children waiting for her.

But it wasn't enough.

"It finally reached a point where I was unwilling to continue my life the way it was," she said the other day. "I wanted to get my mind going."

So Mrs. Jennison, the fashionable-looking wife of a Wall Street money manager, decided to go back to college.

> "When Husband and Home Are Not Enough, Some Women Find Returning to College Is," by Judy Klemesrud, *The New York Times,* February 2, 1975.

"Why do I work so hard? The fact is that I am not conscious of working especially hard, or of 'working' at all. . . . Writing and teaching have always been, for me, so richly rewarding that I do not think of them as work in the usual sense of the word. 'Work' seems to have an aura of obligation or necessity about it, as a term; it often suggests that one is working for money, or for personal gain of some kind, rather than doing something for the sake of it, for pleasure."

> Joyce Carol Oates, novelist, as quoted by Charlotte Curtis, *The New York Times,* March 30, 1975.

He'd been personnel manager for ten years, then corporate secretary, and now, as vice president-administration, he was on top committees and managing a division with a $5-million budget.

He could see that his job might *shrink* a little under the new management— and he was right. In fact, about eighteen months after the merger, it shrank straight off the organization chart and he was told that his terminal leave was about to begin.

. . . Nobody was saying so straight out, but his age was getting in the way— and so was his impressive professional record. "All my badges of success," he began to realize, "were now my greatest liability. Nearly twenty-eight years with the same company, an officer of the company, good salary. All the things you thought were an asset were just the opposite." The power and pay of his old job only scared people off. They questioned him if he'd settle for less. He was locked into his high bracket. His options narrowed to a slit, "Over qualified" was a turndown he came to hate.

> "An Executive Odyssey: Looking for a Job at 55" by Anne Chamberlain, *Fortune*, November 1974.

CHARLEY: Nobody dast blame this man. You don't understand: Willy was a salesman. And for a salesman, there is no rock bottom to the life. He don't put a bolt to a nut, he don't tell you the law or give you the medicine. He's the man way out there in the blue riding on a smile and a shoeshine. And when they start not smiling back—that's an earthquake. And then you get yourself a couple of spots on your hat, and you're finished. Nobody dast blame this man. A salesman is got to dream, boy. It comes with the territory.

> *Death of a Salesman.*

Three weeks from now I'll be seventy-five years old. . . .
   I was a shipping clerk for twenty-five long years. The firm went kerflooey. Then I put in fifteen years at a felt works. I was operating a cutting machine.
   The day goes pretty fast for me now. I don't regret it at all that I've got all this time on hand. I'm enjoying it to the best of my ability. I don't daydream at all. I just think of something and I forget it. That daydreaming don't do you any good. What the heck, there's no reason to have a grouch on or be mad at the world. Smile and the world smiles with you, that's an old slogan.
   I live on a pension and social security. I don't get much pension because I only put in fifteen years at that place. I get thirty-six dollars a month from there and I get $217 from Social Security. If I manage my money, I'm fifteen, twenty dollars to the good every end of the month. I do most of my cooking.

> "Ex-Shipping Clerk" in *Working* by Studs Terkel (New York: Pantheon, 1974).

Man, unlike any other thing organic or inorganic in the universe, grows beyond his work, walks up the stairs of his concepts, emerges ahead of his accomplishments.

> *Grapes of Wrath* by John Steinbeck (New York: Viking Press, 1939).

# In Brief

As this Prospectus goes to press, in mid-1975, more than 4 million men and women in the United States—adults, through with school—are looking for work but can't find it. About $13.5 billion will be paid by the end of fiscal 1975 in unemployment insurance benefits. A concern grows in the country unlike anything in memory: that in the future there will not be enough to do in America for people who depend on work for a living.

This could seem a wrong time to talk of "enriching" education and work, of career education and guidance and counseling, and now in this part of more adult education, of work sabbatics, and of improving the quality of work.

On the contrary.

If the true picture of the future were bleak, the prospect should be made clear *now* to the millions of young Americans who are preparing themselves for a different one.

As for those billions of dollars in unemployment insurance benefits, they are being paid to people who have nothing to do and hate it. In other countries not unlike ours, the adversity of unusual unemployment is at least a little improved upon by increased offerings of training and educational opportunity. Indeed, as we turn to increased "public employment" programs there is new reason to consider the different countercyclical policies in Western European countries that recognize periods of economic contraction as favorable times for significantly enlarged *retraining* programs. When large numbers of workers are torn from their jobs, these countries capitalize on the increased availability of instructional resources and move to meet the great need for those displaced to have purposeful, productive activity, instituting income-support programs to provide living expenses during the adjustment period. These training and adult education programs are then cut back—even below normal—in periods of unusual economic activity and consequent larger demand for labor.

Assuming continuation of present economic policies, today's concern over the long-range employment prospect is valid. For these policies have depended on supplies of natural resources that are being rapidly depleted. The question has to be faced whether this means less work to be done, or larger development of the resources that people, workers, represent. This prospect is not yet clear. But the second alternative surely argues for consideration of what a fuller interrelating of education and training and work as a lifetime process would mean.

Today's prospect has a third dimension. There are clear and unmistakable signs of a new insistence in this country that larger attention be paid to improving the *quality* of life. What an irony it would have been if the wings of this new aspiration had been clipped because of a cutback in our oil supplies and the rationing of some of the other raw materials that we had depended on for growth.

But it won't work out this way. This insistence on the importance of life's finer sense is real. We are already looking for the better ways to keep our new purpose in flight than by expanding the Gross National Product *as we have previously thought of it*. The interesting irony will prove to be that we were pushed faster by new necessity along the course of saner purpose—just as we were required by that same oil shortage to slow up our suicidal careening along the highways, which we now accept as simply good sense.

It is part of this search for new meaning that we are looking for new ways to improve the quality of working life that are not dependent on the stimulant, which had become a narcotic, of a commitment to attain each year the grossest national product in history or in the world.

In view of this new purpose, it is important to be as clear as possible about what we really want from work, what we count as its values and proper uses. Chapter 5 explores this as the essential basis for firm consideration of whether, and how, these values and uses may better be served by a different relating of education and work.

Chapter 6 then reviews the already established *base* of adult education in the United States but draws on comparisons with experience in other countries to suggest how this base may be further built upon.

In Chapter 7 consideration is given to a number of possibilities for developing education and work as more closely coordinated functions—involving, on the one hand, the development of a broad concept of educational renewal opportunity and, on the other, fuller consideration of those elements in the work process itself that relate both to the importance of labor as a unit of production and to the enhancement of work as a human value.

There is finally, in Chapter 8, a consideration of what an education-work policy would mean in the particular circumstances of three large groupings of people: women, "minorities," and all of us as we get older.

# 5.
# Through the Looking Glass

Although our talk of education and work as "two worlds" implies a balance and reciprocity, we, in fact, accord work the infinitely larger authority. If relationships between the two break down, the immediate and often the only reaction is that some adjustment be made in the tributary state of education.

One implication of this is in a sense ironic. The conception of education's purpose as being in significant part to prepare people for work has the effect of seeming to answer any question about its value and to afford a satisfying measure of its success. Superficially, there seems to be a similarly identifiable value in work—to make a living—and a comparable measure, too, of its accomplishment—staying ahead of the Joneses and increasing the Gross National Product. Yet there is, in fact, just enough of the philosopher in most of us, and little enough of the economist, that we question, as we do not about education, whether this all adds up. Willing to work in order to live, we begin to wonder uneasily if we might not be living, instead, to work.

These doubts commend the consideration of another view. This is, in short, that work as presently consitututed does *not* make maximum practical sense—and, further, that both work itself and the broader adult experience can be significantly enriched by what education can mean beyond its traditional preparatory offering.

Only by understanding what it is we want from work—what we mean by it and what we want it to mean—can we understand and evaluate whatever a broader, longer, and more influential education might have to offer.

To begin with, our expressed attitudes toward work are full of contradictions. The necessity imposed by cold and hunger *forces* most of us to seek paid employment; yet we present ourselves as *eager* to "earn our own way." Although our collective anxiety about what would happen if our own paychecks stopped coming has led to protections such as unemployment insurance and welfare, many among us condemn people "on unemployment" as undeserving. We recognize work as vital to life and ego, yet heated political controversy ensues whenever there is insufficient work to go around, and it is proposed that government intervene to create jobs for the unemployed. Work presents both a chance for success, which will be recognized by friends and neighbors, and a chance for failure, which may cause despondency and feelings of personal inadequacy. Failure at work can lead to the psychiatrist's office, where, ironically, the patient just leaving is being eased *into* employment to increase feelings of adequacy and personal fulfillment.

To look back on history is to find only a compounding of these confusions. The importance of work has varied over time and from place to place, a fact to keep in mind lest we take too seriously any prevailing attitude, in an America a mere two centuries old, that work processes as we currently know them are an unalterable condition of human existence.

Whatever moved civilized society away from the Athenian idea that work is servile and degrading to the view that hard work is the route to salvation is now dim cultural memory. To use John Kenneth Galbraith's phrase, the Christian or the Protestant—but perhaps even more so the American—"work ethic" comes down to the identification of work as a convenient social virtue without which the Industrial Revolution could never have amassed the wealth of nations. Our belief in the virtue of work came before the need for people to operate the new machines, but no one would question that the exaltation of work is intertwined with the rise of capitalism and the accompanying sunburst of new economic opportunities.

So there is no identifiable basis for talking about work objectively from any fixed starting point of common beliefs.

Despite this lack of a timeworthy concept of the place of work in life, there is a persistent and on the whole pervasive notion that the conditions of work have, over time, improved.

Even this gives the philosopher pause. Improvement is so much in the eye of the beholder. How does one compare the wrestling of one stone onto the top of another to build a great pyramid with gripping a pneumatic drill that is pounding into the asphalt of today's city street? In his history of England, Trevelyan quotes a plowman of a thousand years ago:

... hard do I work ... at daybreak driving the oxen to field ... Nor is it ever so hard a winter that I dare loiter at home ... Then ... I must fill the bin of the oxen with hay and water and carry out the dung.

How would this strike one of today's tenant farmers trying to eke a living from marginal land? How would the plowman compare his plight to that of a coal miner, hunched in the dark, three or four feet from floor to ceiling, with dust to breathe and the beginnings of a cough he now knows by the name of black lung?

As we moved into the Industrial Revolution, even who did what in the world of enterprise shifted. England used children in the new factories. Chroniclers of the current movement for bringing women into what is too often considered men's work may have forgotten that the American answer to the machines' demands was women. It was the Lowell factory girls of 1840 of whom Cochran and Miller wrote, in their *Age of Enterprise:*[1]

The great mass wear out their health, spirits and morals without becoming one whit better off than when they commenced their labor. The bills of mortality in these factory villages are not striking, we admit, for the poor girls when they can toil no longer go home to die.

Perhaps it can be argued with reasonable confidence that the emergence of a professional, managerial, and technical class of jobs, carrying with them a special prestige, indicates that we must have made at least some significant improvements in job quality. Yet, even here, as Walter Neff points out in *The Social Dimensions of Work,* "all useful work in the Greek city-states—even the occupations related to trade and education—were performed by slaves, serfs, and outlander citizens."[2] Plainly, each time and place has its own hierarchy of rankings of what constitutes "good" work. Nothing is likely to be gained by skipping through history for examples of what the common person did to ward off the elements except to prove the vulnerabilty of any simple statement about what has happened to jobs and to challenge the assumption that the changes have benefited the people who perform them. For a very large number of workers, what has probably changed more than the content of jobs is the circumstances under which they are performed, the time involved, and the betterment in nonwork life made possible by an advancing economy. Commonly, progress has been defined in terms of how much earnings can be taken from work and how much time can be spent away from it. We point with pride to the fact of a constant reduction in this country of the work week—confused only by the companion fact that corporate and government decision-makers, doctors, engineers, and lawyers are working longer and longer days and accepting it, even displaying it, as a measure of their importance. The material rewards from work seem ever to advance, even when, as in recent years, they are overtaken by faster rising prices. The slowly but steadily growing strength of unions has restricted the power of employers to terminate a person's livelihood without good cause; a worker has earned the right both to an occasional bad day on the job and to be protected from the capricious decisions of a boss made irritable by a poor night's sleep.

But for all that has been said about the improvement in working conditions in the United States, few observers have confronted the issue of the content or meaning of work itself. Have jobs become more onerous? Or more fulfilling? Is work giving wider scope for the exercise of the human intellect? On these questions little research has been done. Indeed, in the broad perspective of history, they hardly seem worth asking. But in a time of generalized concern with the quality of life they become increasingly relevant questions and, although of inherent complexity, to be taken seriously—lest we become, as Eric Heller fears we may have already, "so democratic in our habits of thought that we are convinced that truth is determined through a plebiscite of facts."

Admittedly, when the question, "Has the content of work for the average person improved?" is posed in the context of history, there may be no answer. The value of that content is perceived differently at different times and cannot be abstracted from the culture in which the work is performed. But what about more recent history, say the United States in the last quarter century?

Confining the question helps some, but present measures are not very good for this purpose either. We can look at gross changes in job distributions by the way they are classified by the government, roughly designed to reflect prestige rankings. The table on page 88 shows changes in job distribution for men and women over the twenty-five-year period between 1948 and 1973.[3]

These statistics show only one significant shift in the distribution of jobs for men—the decline in farm jobs—over the last quarter century, with most of this decline being taken up in the increase in professional and technical jobs. Otherwise, and contrary to popular belief, there has been virtual stability of the occupational mix over that extended period during which technological advance was rampant and we were moving rapidly toward a service economy.

To judge from the data, given present American attitudes toward the better occupation, a higher percentage of the work force seems to have been boosted into prestigious professional and technical jobs. At the same time, the opportunity to be the most independent of American workers—the owner of a farm—has steadily eroded. Otherwise, little change is discernible for men, and what change has occurred for women is hard to interpret beyond the clear advantage associated with the decline in the necessity to work as maids in other people's houses.

|  | (Percentage Distribution) | | | |
|  | 1948 | | 1973 | |
|  | *Male* | *Female* | *Male* | *Female* |
| *White Collar* | | | | |
| Professional and technical | 5.8% | 9.0% | 13.6% | 14.5% |
| Managers and administrators except farm | 12.8 | 5.2 | 13.6 | 4.9 |
| Sales workers | 5.3 | 8.2 | 6.1 | 6.9 |
| Clerical workers | 6.9 | 26.9 | 6.6 | 34.3 |
| *Blue Collar* | | | | |
| Craftsmen, foremen, kindred | 18.7 | 1.2 | 20.8 | 1.4 |
| Operatives and kindred | 21.1 | 20.5 | 18.8 | 13.8 |
| Laborers, except farm and mine | 7.8 | .5 | 7.7 | .9 |
| *Service Workers* | | | | |
| Private household | .4 | 9.5 | — | 4.1 |
| Other | 5.8 | 11.0 | 7.9 | 17.5 |
| *Farm Workers* | | | | |
| Farmers and managers | 10.4 | 1.6 | 3.0 | .3 |
| Farm laborers and foremen | 5.0 | 6.5 | 1.8 | 1.3 |

An analysis based on the gross occupational classifications of the Bureau of the Census is admittedly shaky, for these classifications are highly aggregated and do not adequately reveal changing job content.

More sophisticated studies, however, confirm the fact that during the past quarter century there has been only a minimal rise in the skill content of jobs within homogeneous skill clusters,[4] and little if any in the educational development required for them.[5] The relationship between skill levels and educational development is shown in the chart below.

| Level of Job | Years of General Educational Development | |
|---|---|---|
| | 1940 | 1970 |
| I | 16.31 | 16.11 |
| II | 12.01 | 12.17 |
| III | 10.54 | 10.43 |
| IV | 9.75 | 9.43 |
| V | 7.85 | 7.96 |

Yet, the mean educational attainment level of the U.S. labor force (eighteen to sixty-four years old) rose from 8.6 years for men and 9.8 years for women in 1940 to 12.0 years for men and 12.1 years for women in 1973.[6] In short, work today calls on a good deal less of the education that people are able to bring to it. This disparity is increasing rapidly. What does it portend?

A fairly widespread effort has been exerted recently to find out more about the work situation by attempted analyses of worker satisfaction and a concomitant concentration of attention on the quality of work. This was stimulated particularly by concerns that arose in the late 1960s and early 1970s, when inflation had brought real wages to a virtual standstill. The consequent squeeze was resulting in worker discontent and even a digging in against continued progress in removing barriers to establishing equality of employment opportunity.

These attempts at survey and statistical analysis have so far produced perhaps more questions than answers; but this is plainly part of the discovery process. The results of one of these surveys, carried out by the Michigan Survey Research Center under Department of Labor funding, were publicized in a volume by Sheppard and Herrick entitled *Where Have All the Robots Gone?*[7] Their interpretation of the data is implied in the title and in their labeling of Part I, *The Myth of the Happy Worker:* Workers are no longer going to put up with the monotony of assembly lines. One out of every five workers surveyed expressed negative attitudes toward work. Younger workers were found to be most discontented with their lot, and by and large those groups getting the least from their employment expressed the most dissatisfaction with it.

There were other reports and developments in this same pattern: Gallup polls that showed worker satisfaction going up but then down when a different sample was used; reports of increasing turnover rates, absenteeism, and industrial sabotage; and the Lordstown strike at the new GM Vega plant, widely publicized at the time as an expression of new militancy among young workers, but more responsibly identified later as a traditional walkout triggered by a speedup.[8] During the same period increasing reports came from Europe of significant results from experiments with "job redesign" and "job enrichment," especially in Scandinavia.

The attitude surveys, linked with the experimental approaches and then with yet a third strand of psychologically based theories such as Maslow's "hierarchy of needs," soon defined an area of concern commonly expressed as "the quality of work."

Recent analyses suggest strongly that while it is probably correct that between a tenth and a fifth of American workers are dissatisfied with their work, this is about the way it has been for at least for some time now.[9] A 1973 rerun of a 1969 national survey was reported as showing "no change in overall job satisfaction between 1969 and 1973," with the further indication that this was equally the case in "subpopulations distinguished according to sex, age, race, education, employment status (self-employed versus wage and salary) and collar color."[10] The most recent and thorough analysis of the historical data concludes that "there has been no substantial change in overall levels of job satisfaction over the last decade."[11] A probably significant exception to this pattern is in one study that finds that the percent of noncollege youth who "believe that hard work always pays off" declined from 79 percent in 1969 to 56 percent in 1973.[12]

There have apparently been no significant changes in worker contentment as it may be reflected in terms of job turnover, absenteeism, strikes, and productivity, although these analyses have been based on aggregate statistics that would not show any newly emerging conditions among particular segments of the labor force or in particular industries.[13]

Given these survey results, and taking account of the rising level of education in the work force, the better question would seem to be, "Why are there so many robots still around?" But that, too, would miss the point. What is important, and must be gotten at in some way, is the question of what the meaningfulness of work really is. The pollsters' questions are put, and the answers are given, in terms of words infected with the bias of custom and the conditioning of attitudes.

It may well be that the largest significance of this recent round of polling is in its revealing that the answers to questions about people's satisfaction or dissatisfaction about their work parallel almost precisely their answers about their feelings regarding life in general. Sheppard and Herrick have set this out:[14]

|  | Negative Attitudes Toward Work (%) | Negative Attitudes Toward Life (%) |
|---|---|---|
| Race |  |  |
| Black | 23 | 21 |
| White | 14 | 12 |
| Age |  |  |
| Under 20 | 25 | 20 |
| 20—29 | 24 | 14 |
| 30—44 | 13 | 15 |
| 45—54 | 11 | 10 |
| 55 and older | 6 | 10 |
| Occupation |  |  |
| Professional, technical, and managerial | 9 | 10 |
| Clerical and sales | 18 | 14 |
| Service | 23 | 24 |
| Machine trades | 15 | 11 |
| Structure work | 10 | 7 |
| Sex |  |  |
| Male | 12 | 12 |
| Female | 19 | 17 |

There has been no definitive analysis of which way—as between work and other life elements—cause and effect run here. It is, so far, only like the equation of the chemical reaction: a double set of arrows pointing in opposite directions. But this isn't an ultimate answer, and there is more to be found out about this before we settle on trying to do something about job design alone.

What does it mean if four out of five say they are satisfied with their work? Compared with what? Maurice Chevalier replied ruefully, when he was asked what it felt like to be eighty, "Pretty good in view of the alternative."

We *accept* work as one of the elements to be lived with, as farmers live with the inevitable droughts that mar their livelihood. We do what we must and adjust to what we are conditioned to think we can't change—including the pact that tradition insists was made long ago between people and material progress—that progress can be had, as long as people do what the production system requires. When you ask us, in a survey, whether we are satisfied, do you mean are we content? Do you ask about the quality of our work or about us? Is your question whether we think we have won our battle or are losing it, or only whether we are willing to go along with the armistice—some "peace with honor" arrangement?

A few, Daniel Yankelovich notably among them, have at least started to illuminate the psychological dimension of work.[15] Family heads judge themselves as they are judged by others—by their competence as breadwinners. A seemingly simple question about satisfaction with the job will be colored by the image a person holds of how well he or she is meeting the expectations of family and friends, which touches on identity. Being somebody and successfully maneuvering through the economic world get bound into one question: "Have you failed in life or succeeded?" The second query on meeting an old friend is always, "What are you *doing* now?" Yet if so far the head counters and psychologists have brought back no clear answers from their pioneering efforts, they have encouraged us anew to ask questions.

One thing we know. The *nature* of jobs is changing significantly, and with a consistent diminishing effect on the requirement of purely physical input. Machines now do most of what used to be the most common, that is, the meanest, hard labor—at least by tradition's measurement. In oil refineries, what jobs remain have become increasingly the watching of gauges to see that the machines are behaving, and the turning of wheels for corrective adjustments. Bank tellers dial the account number before cashing a check, rather than looking up the piece of paper that used to carry the customer's current balance. Yet the net of all this is hard to judge, for the human implications of gauge-watching or of cradling princess-style telephones at bank windows have not yet been assessed.

While the machine occupies center stage in any discussion of the changing character of production and jobs, organizational technology takes prominent billing, too. It was the layout of the store that changed the grocer's job from searching the shelves for items on a customer's shopping list, adding up the cost, and bagging to just adding *or* bagging *or* stocking. We remain in the dark about whether the larger job in a corner grocery (why can't the customers decide whether they want pork or beef roast for Sunday?) or the specialized job in a supermarket (always another cart emptied onto the counter before the prior order is totaled) is more rewarding to the human spirit.

There is, on the other hand, the significantly increased prospect now that people will move, in the course of their work careers, from one type of job to another largely because some types of jobs are expanding and others diminishing. This is particularly true with respect to women, for there has been more change in the types of jobs available to them than in those for men, although the similarities are more noticeable than the differences. Yet here again we know nothing about the broader significance, in terms of human fulfillment, of such change. Except in the clear instance of women's enlarged opportunities, we don't even know how much of it involves freedom of choice on the one hand or compulsion on the other.

So, in general, job content is changing but we don't know whether, in the language of social science questionnaires, we are consequently "worse off," "better off," or "about the same"—or even whether we are at all clear about the meaning of these terms in relation to work.

Today, almost suddenly, a new dimension is being added to this picture of job or work change. Now there is developing, for really the first time on any significant scale, an initiative for *purposive* change in jobs, the purpose being to make them more satisfying and meaningful to those performing them.

This prospect has been caught best, clearly before the flood, of recent interest, in the notable 1972 report, *Work in America,* commissioned by the then Secretary of Health, Education, and Welfare.[16]

Because work is central to the lives of so many Americans, either the absence of work or employment in meaningless work is creating an intolerable situation. The human costs of this state of affairs are manifested in worker alienation, alcoholism, drug addiction and other symptoms of poor mental health. Moreover, much of our tax money is expended in an effort to compensate for problems with at least a part of their genesis in the world of work. . . . the essential first step is the commitment on the part of policy makers in business, labor, and government to the improvement of the quality of working life in America.

The initiatives developed in this area reflect a broad range of purposes, involving most particularly various combinations of interest in (1) improving the lives of American workers by enriching the quality of work, and (2) increasing productivity.

So far the actual experiments conducted in American industry have been done largely on an internal basis. Significant evaluation by independent outside agencies is only now getting started, most of it under the auspices of the Department of Labor and the National Commission on Productivity and Work Quality. Meanwhile, what seem to be straightforward efforts to restructure jobs to make them more fulfilling are being viewed with a general skepticism that in some quarters edges toward hostility. This is true partly because of the complexity of motivations, partly because of the ways the ideas have been brought forward, and partly because of the formidable task implicit in any major restructuring of the American industrial system. No forward movement will be possible unless these factors are better understood.

This effort and these prospects cannot be isolated from the concerns of the American labor movement. Workers and their jobs are the essence of what unions are about. Unions, since their inception, have concerned themselves with working conditions, pay, hours of work, fringe benefits, grievance procedures, representation in general, and other agenda items not easily distinguishable from whatever is meant to be implied by "quality of work." It is the unfortunate fact that unprincipled opportunists have tried to exploit these new approaches as effective "union busting" tactics. Because increased productivity is unquestionably a principal, and entirely legitimate, concern of many management participants in these job enrichment and job redesign efforts, there will be a natural tendency among union leaders to suspect these as being merely more elegant names for the old-fashioned speed-up—one more way to exact higher profits from the eight-hour day.

It will be unfortunate if the initial tendency toward a polarization of attitudes persists. The different meanings of quality of work to employees and employers are in no sense inherently inconsistent. On the contrary. There is plainly a constructive purpose here that in no way conflicts with organized labor's objectives, and an approach that can parallel and complement, indeed be part of, traditional representation and collective bargaining processes. Experience-seasoned government and other public representatives are already engaged, in cooperation with both labor and management leaders, in establishing a firmer basis for exploring this prospect further.

This won't be an easy undertaking, especially as it moves past the experimental stage. Part of the success of the Industrial Revolution was in the breaking apart of jobs into separate tasks, each defined in its own terms and with little regard to monotony's effect on the human psyche. Employers, no less than unions, will have their doubts: about how a new plant layout can be made to accommodate the presumed desire of workers without playing havoc with parts delivery systems, and about what job changes for some vague purpose of human fulfillment will do to unit costs and profit-and-loss statements. Crippling personnel shortages on the assembly lines in extremely tight labor markets were clearly the impelling force behind job redesign experiments in Europe. American employers have not faced labor markets this tight in recent history. Which is not to say they will *not* be receptive, only that there are no such clear and strong economic forces at work in the United States to make them receptive. Indeed, a time of eight to ten percent unemployment, and of increased struggle to keep real wages from dropping further than they already have, is not a propitious season for the growth of new interest in the quality of work—although fuller reason would very properly argue otherwise.

Granted that any significant reordering of the workplace will face formidable barriers, it remains nevertheless almost unarguably worthwhile to encourage programs and efforts calculated to make the content of jobs more rewarding to the people performing them. Such programs are needed despite, perhaps because of, the intrinsic structural problems and the troublesome ambiguities in attitude currently reported among union leaders, employers, and workers themselves. Modern behavioral research has now confirmed a rationale once advanced only by poets and worldly philosophers:

Albert Camus: "A face that toils so close to stones is already stone itself." More than might seem desirable, what one does determines who one is.

Adam Smith: "The very different genius which appears to distinguish men of different professions, when grown to maturity, is not upon many occasions so much the cause as the effect of the division of labor." It is the content of work that usually fixes the worker's place in the hierarchy of approval.

In perhaps more pragmatic terms it is by no means even suggested in the evidence so far that the creation of more challenging jobs means higher per unit labor costs or that it is inimical to increased acceleration in the per capita GNP. The indications are, rather, the opposite. And if the human resource must be more fully drawn on in the future than it has been in a past characterized by irrational uses of now more precious natural resources, a larger consideration of labor's meaning to those offering it seems a fair part of the bargain.

What is it, then, that can be said about work?

- That there is, first, a web of seemingly conflicting and contradictory attitudes about the essential place of work in life beyond the primary need to provide the means of sustenance.
- That we think in terms of "improvement" in the conditions and circumstances of work and share some rough sense that there *is* improvement, though we are less than certain what this means or actually amounts to.
- That there is at the same time a consciousness of an increasing dissatisfaction with something about work, but that this, too, gets less clear the harder it is looked at.
- That there are material changes going on in the nature of work, but no clear indications yet of the consequent differences, if any, in work's meaning to the worker.
- And that a new, and potentially significant, concentration of attention on the quality of work has contributed, so far, as much to controversy as to comprehension.

What has education to do with this?

One element in this uncertain picture has particular, if only illustrative, relevance. The American commitment to education, and the faith we have placed in education as the route to position in the meritocracy, are providing an ever more highly educated labor force—more high school graduates, more college graduates, more advanced degrees. But we are developing more highly educated people faster than we are creating jobs that traditionally required this much education. Inherent in this disparity are degrees of overqualification, underemployment, and social discontent probably without precedent. On the face of it this seems to spell trouble. Yet, the disparity implies a promise that reaches infinitely beyond the threat. If viewed not as preparation for work but as *part* of work and of the larger life experience, education offers at least some of the answer to the confusions and contradictions and ambiguities that have so confounded us.

Next, then, of lifetime education.

# 6.
# The Who and What of Adult Education

For a long time, work's claim on life was bounded for most people simply by their *capacity* to work. It took all they had. Children got a few years' schooling, but time in the schoolhouse was carefully tailored to the work demands at home and on the farm. Older people worked until their bodies gave out. This was all there was to it.

We only half realize the extent to which this almost total dominion of work over life has gradually been broken: by extending youths' schooling, by cutting the number of hours in industry's work year almost in half, by a sharp reduction in the average number of children per family, by fixing earlier and earlier retirement ages, and by extending our longevity. Transferring a good deal of work's physical rigors to machines has meant a comparably significant reduction in its drain on human energies. The net of it is that work takes less than half as much of life's waking hours as it did a century ago and gives us more than twice the opportunity for other uses.

We have done astonishingly little with this dividend. We hardly even realize that we have it. Perhaps there is something in the psychology of our financial dependence on earning a living that keeps our thinking about life's broadened opportunities in a continuing but now illusory bondage. Perhaps it is something else. But it seems a mistake.

Part of the strangeness of the reaction, or lack of it, to this development is that as three stages of life have emerged more distinctly we have categorized their appointed functions so sharply: youth for education, adulthood for work, old age for "retirement."

Any seventeen-year-old not in school is a dropout, any healthy forty-year-old not at work a laggard, and any seventy-year-old still at work an anomaly.

It is part of this same categorization of function that with respect to adulthood generally the substantially lessened demands of work on the time and energy of people between the ages of twenty and sixty have resulted as little as they have in the use of these released hours and energies for education—despite education's unquestionable continuing attraction, and manifest advantage, to a great many of us. This seems worth looking at more closely.

There have been, particularly in very recent years, obviously significant developments in "adult education." By and large, however, these programs have developed more by impulse than by plan, emerging not from a broad policy and purpose but from quite narrow and specific concerns. Generally, the movement has been tied closely to the work purpose. The official U.S. Government Survey defines adult education as something done part-time, reflecting the assumption that it complements the full-time activity of work. Much of what is now offered and taken is for improving productivity *on the present job* or meeting certification requirements for salary advancement.

There is one important exception to this. For unique reasons, we have provided education—years of it and full-time—to 15 million military veterans as partial adjustment for having interrupted their lives and exposed them to the risk of death. Few question the justice of this or its value to the recipients, their families, and society.

As of this writing, Congress has yet to vote on the possibility of a cutoff date for eligibility for GI Bill benefits, in light of the fact that we no longer have a military draft in this country. The Carnegie Council on Policy Studies, however, has recommended that the principle of the GI Bill be applied to situations where educational benefits are awarded for a defined period of community service.

## ADULT LEARNERS: HOW MANY AND WHAT FOR?

The difficulty of deciding who is to be considered an adult and what kind of learning is to be considered education has resulted in varying, even strange, estimates of how many "adults" are getting "education." In 1972 the United States Office of Education reported 15.7 million adults participating in education,[1] defining them as

all individuals, in the civilian population, past compulsory school attendance age who participate in part-time educational activities organized around some form of instruction.

Thus, the seventeen-year-old high school dropout going to barbering school at night is included—an adult. A twenty-eight-year-old still in school studying a specialized branch of medicine is not. The survey picks up an evening yoga class at the YMCA but leaves out veterans going to school full-time. Adults are counted only when they fit into the educational pattern expected of working adults.* Others have attempted a more complete count. The 1973 Carnegie Commission report, *Toward a Learning Society,* concluded that in 1970 there were approximately 57 million people in higher and other postsecondary education, most of them over eighteen years and therefore legally adults. Even such expanded estimates "do not include participation in self-study, independent study related to organized instruction, and informal learning activities at home, on the job, or elsewhere." While having the advantage of comprehensiveness, many of the estimates would be extremely difficult to substantiate.

These counts, moreover, are of questionable utility. For example, under "employers and associations," 15.7 million are described as receiving "safety instruction"; on analysis, this turns out to be a group who are occasionally assembled in their place of employment to be told how to avoid injury in the workplace and what to do in plant emergencies. The anomaly of such a figure is suggested by the next statistic in the table—7.4 million receiving "job orientation." This is the only—though misleading—clue offered to the amount of job training given by U.S. employers to their employees. Because of the informal nature of the bulk of job training in American enterprise, such training has never been adequately measured; indeed, employers infrequently keep records.[2]

If one accepts the premise that adult education is something done largely part-time, the best profile of its participants is probably contained in the well designed U.S. Office of Education Survey. According to its findings, three out of four part-time students are under forty-five, and one third are within the age span of twenty-five to thirty-four.[3] Fifty percent of the adult education enrollees

---

*Returning Peace Corps volunteers and finishing VISTA volunteers resuming full-time education are excluded from this count, as are women and older people who return full-time to the education system. Regardless of age, all full-time participants in proprietary—that is, for profit—schools are excluded, as well as full-time participants in manpower, vocational education, and apprenticeship programs.

surveyed, compared to 19 percent among the nonenrollees in the sample, had at least some college education. Only 13 percent of the adult education participants had less than a high school education, compared to 43 percent of the nonparticipants. Plainly, those who already *have* education are getting more.

Given the greater education of the participants, it is not surprising that they also come from families with higher incomes. Sixty-one percent of the participants have family incomes above $10,000, compared to 41 percent of the nonparticipants.

The purposes these participating adults reportedly expect to accomplish vary considerably. For many, it is to raise skill levels; for others it is to acquire new knowledge and perspective about self and society; for some it is to meet other people; for yet others it is to acquire the credits or credentials necessary for retaining or advancing in their jobs; for others it is to fulfill recreational, entertainment, or leisure-time needs.

When asked what their primary purpose was, the most common response (43 percent) was that they wanted to improve or advance in their jobs. Eleven percent were attending in order to get a new job, 16 percent were there for general information, 23 percent for personal development and household management, and 6 percent for social and recreational purposes.

The kind of educational activities adults enroll in parallel the interests that support these activities financially. It would be a mistake to take the existing situation as representative of what people would want if financing sources supported a wider array of options.

In 1972 employers paid for all or part of the education of more than 4 million adults in part-time education programs. As an employer, the federal government is the single largest provider, financing almost 1 million adult education opportunities for its employees each year.[4] Public funds, provided mostly through the continuing education provision of various pieces of categorical legislation, finance an additional 2.8 million part-time adult education opportunities; much of this is to encourage continued skill improvement in the professions—especially health, social service, law enforcement, and education.[5] Even when the education is self-financed, the professions often force continuing education by making salary increases or continued certification conditional on it. Pay raises for teachers are commonly geared to the completion of work for advanced degrees. In a few states doctors are required to keep up with new medical developments in order to have their licenses renewed. The bar associations, through continuing legal education are giving more and more attention to periodic relicensing.

To be sure, a significant number of adults fund their own part-time education, solely for the purpose of pleasure and the widening of their knowledge. And there are adults, largely in the narrow bands at the higher income levels, who are able to go to school full time for the same reasons.

Four-year colleges still garner the most adults but the great current expansion is in the two-year colleges—at growth rates that could push these colleges above all other forms within a few years. Only modest expansions in part-time education are occurring at the high schools, and in the private vocational schools adult enrollments are not gaining at all.

Adult Education by Source, 1969 and 1972

(participants in millions)

| | 1969 | 1972 | Percent Change |
|---|---|---|---|
| Public grade school or high school | 1.9 | 2.2 | +12 |
| Two-year college or technical institute | 1.6 | 2.6 | +65 |
| Private vocational, trade, or business school | 1.5 | 1.4 | - 7 |
| Four-year college or university | 2.8 | 3.4 | +19 |
| Employer | 2.3 | 2.6 | +15 |
| Other (unions, professional associations, hospitals, tutors) | 2.6 | 3.4 | +32 |
| (Not reported) | .1 | .1 | — |
| | 13.0 | 15.7 | +21 |

Source: Surveys by the U.S. Office of Education

A spurt of growth is coming from the unions and professional associations as, increasingly, education for employees is placed on the bargaining table. In the last complete count made by the Bureau of Labor Statistics (1969), 344 collective bargaining contracts (out of a total of 1823 major contracts) contained specific training agreements. Of those, fifty-two provided for tuition aid, the remainder for on-the-job training.[6] More recent BLS information on agreements in manufacturing establishments with 1000 or more employees, suggests a significant growth in those collective bargaining efforts. In 1972 there were 1300 such agreements covering 6.3 million workers: 565 in apprenticeship and 519 in on-the-job training, 34 providing for a "training fund" contributed to by the employer, and 88 providing tuition aid.[7]

The range of effort is considerable. The AFL-CIO now has a Labor Studies Center with a wide array of educational offerings and has recently begun an "external degree" program in cooperation with Antioch College. For about a decade, under a contract between employers and the Seafarers International Union, employers have contributed to an educational fund for minorities and the disadvantaged. The Blacklake Center in Michigan, begun by Walter Reuther, is a residential "family education center" for union members, centering on labor education but only slightly less concerned with the workings of the political and economic systems.

Employer-provided tuition-refund programs, the great majority of which are not likely to be encompassed by collective bargaining agreements, are undoubtedly growing, but there is no presently available record of them. To an increasing degree in large corporations, such plans are becoming established avenues for promotion.

In the 1960s the government added a new dimension to adult education by passing the Manpower Development and Training Act of 1962 and the Economic Opportunity Act of 1964, both of which provided retraining opportunities for the poor and the unemployed. While those efforts tended to peak fast, by fiscal year 1973 they amounted to only 433,000.[8] With the recent decentralization of manpower responsibilities to local governments, the future of existing efforts is somewhat uncertain, but a good share of what now exists will likely remain—except as current economic pressures may shift these programs more toward employment and away from training.

As difficult as it is to get a good count of participants in formal adult education programs, it is even harder to describe the less formal learning opportunities. For example, in 1962,* agricultural extension agents tallied 4.6 million visits to farms, homes, and offices; almost 8 million office consultations; and 224,000 training sessions for local leaders, attended by 5.2 million people.[9]

Clearly, a lot of adult learning is beyond statistical measurement, but then, living is itself a constant learning process and, with this as given, perhaps it is sufficient that we confine our attention to those *institutional* arrangements expressly directed toward educating adults. In these terms one must conclude that opportunities are

---

*The last year the U.S. Department of Agriculture took a count.

growing but within a rather narrow band. Moreover, the growing opportunities are largely limited to persons who have the most to begin with.

## THE LARGER EXPERIENCE

Conspicuously on the increase are those opportunities for adults variously described as open university or external degree programs. The number of people taking the General Educational Development (GED) examination, a battery of tests certifying competence through the high school level (regardless of formal education), increased from about 39,000 in 1949 to almost 423,000 in 1973. The average GED candidate is twenty-five years old and has had almost ten years of formal education.[10]

Programs verifying the competence of individuals to perform college-level work are similarly expanding, notably through the College-Level Examination Program (CLEP), which administers tests of two kinds: (1) general examinations in English composition, the humanities, the natural sciences, mathematics, and the social sciences; and (2) special-subject examinations in such fields as educational psychology, geology, English composition, statistics, and so on. On the basis of these examinations, decisions are reached as to whether an individual should be granted credit for learning that has occurred outside the established education system. Between June 1974 and May 1975, 35,000 candidates took almost 95,000 CLEP tests, and by mid-1975 more than 1500 institutions had agreed to use the results. More than 50 percent of the candidates taking these tests were twenty or over.[11] Such examining techniques, accompanied by exposure to Great Britain's Open University experiments, have led to an increasing number of innovations with external-degree options. Though the number of participating adults is still fairly small, the trend is decidedly up.

These adult education developments have an international context; many of the models for U.S. policy, programs, and legislation come from a variety of other countries. For example, the Organization for Economic Co-operation and Development (OECD) is establishing a concept called recurrent education that represents an approach with perhaps the most comprehensive set of objectives so far. The OECD explains this concept in far-reaching terms:

The concept of *recurrent education* as it is used in this report expounds the relationship between 'learning' and 'education' by putting it in the perspective of the necessity for a lifelong process of assimilation of new knowledge and experience at the service of a continuous openness to new situations and of enhancing people's ability to take their destiny into their own hands . . . The view is put forward that, because of the complexity of modern society, due in great part to technological development, the need for opportunities to alternate incidental and informal lifelong learning with more organized and intentional educational opportunities is rapidly increasing.[12]

Additionally, it has been mainly through the efforts of the OECD that interest has been generated in such issues as flexible patterns of working time and paid educational leave. To be sure, these initiatives all have their base in particular national settings, the United States being no exception, but the OECD forum has advanced policy discussions materially. A review of its reports discloses serious consideration of some ten to fifteen proposals for various forms of universal access to more education.

In the United States, even though adult participation in education is increasing at rates double those for youth, such increases have occurred largely unaided by a policy framework or by government support. The only exceptions are categorical professional training assistance, the limited retraining under the legislation of the 1960s, and the general aid to the education of veterans. In Europe, where governments have tended to take the initiative, developments have been both more orderly and better focused.[13] Almost inevitably, U.S. attention must soon turn to the need to fashion a coherent policy base for what are so far *ad hoc* efforts. This will lead, as it has in Europe, to a recognition of the new frontiers for both economic and human growth that open up when they are approached jointly by pioneers from the provinces of *both* education and work.

In Germany, for example, the Labor Promotion Act of 1969 provides considerable support now to individuals in vocational training to upgrade their work positions or to adapt to new jobs; it provides aid, as well, to various institutions for expanding vocational education offerings. The legislation was devised primarily to improve the health of the employment market by increasing the vertical and horizontal mobility of the labor force. For the average participating German worker, it means as much as two years in a training, retraining, or education situation—full-time. During this period, the individuals get not only free education but about 70 percent of their former wages. Allowances for partial education are also provided. The law goes beyond providing training and education and includes job-finding assistance. The entire effort is funded through the unemployment insurance system, by a wage tax shared equally by employers and employees.

In 1971 France enacted a comprehensive law that made continuing education for workers a matter of right. Wage earners are eligible to take as much as a year off for training for any of several purposes: preventive unemployment, promotion, obtaining new employment within an industry, or simply for renewal of skills. Employment preparation for unemployed people aged sixteen to eighteen is also provided. Financing is arranged through a wage-related tax on employers, matched by state funds; in 1972 this amounted to 1.25 percent of wages but is expected to rise to 2.0 percent in 1976.[14] The legislation came only after years of negotiation between and among workers' and teachers' trade unions, management, and government. Its adoption is attributable to two causes: a matured recognition of adult education as an important means of helping individuals cope with the pressures of rapid social change, and to what was seen at the time as an existing need of the economy for more skilled workers.

In Sweden extensive adult education and retraining programs have been nurtured in a climate of close working relationships among labor, management, and government. The Swedish Labor Market Board has been granted considerable freedom in determining the dimensions of the education and training effort. It uses that authority as a major instrument in overall economic and employment policy. The Board expands education and training opportunities when economic circumstances necessitate deflation, and reduces such activities when more labor is needed in times of high demand and labor shortages. Such a policy would have significant applicability in the United States today. Economic recession is a time for more training and education, not less. It means that the human resource can be developed, in such periods, at lower cost—because there is less alternative use for it.

Denmark's folk high schools provide perhaps the most flexible form of state-subsidized adult education to be found anywhere. The folk high schools strongly advocate general education instruction, as opposed to a narrow focus on vocational skills. Workers attending receive stipends to cover their personal costs, but no broader support is provided.

Adult education in the United Kingdom has taken two quite different directions. Growing largely out of a concern with productivity and competition in world markets, the United Kingdom encourages worker education through a tax on employers that is reduced or rebated for those employers who provide training themselves and is otherwise collected and used to finance training activities in industrywide facilities. This is done industry by industry through Industry Training Boards that have the power to set the tax rate. Each Board is made up of employers, employees, and educators, chaired by a person with considerable industrial or commercial experience, all appointed by the Minister of Labour.

The United Kingdom's Open University is designed to serve adults holding full-time jobs who want to earn bachelor's degrees. Formally launched in 1971, the Open University is a distinctly off-campus enterprise, with much of the instruction conducted on television and through correspondence. While the initial expectation was that it would mainly serve a working-class clientele, the program thus far has proved most popular with people already in professional and managerial positions.

This brief review of European practice provides only a sketchy basis for assessing the particular relevance of international experience to the situation in the United States. The movement in Europe—at least with respect to occupational training—is clearly toward making it a matter of *right* that government-assisted education be available to all adults. The still broader significance in a comparison of the two sets of developments is that in Europe the expansion of adult education opportunities has proceeded within the context of formulated public policy regarding both education and work, while its growth in this country has so far been essentially only a random response to a variety of market demands.

### THE IMPERATIVES OF CHANGE

This picture of a burgeoning but sprawling development of adult education in the United States must be put beside the picture, sketched out in the preceding chapter, of new gropings toward some more rational and meaningful idea of the place of work in people's lives—for they are closely related. The sense, purpose, and direction lacking in each of them, viewed alone, begin to emerge when the two are seen together.

One reason that so many more adults—new millions each year—are turning to one form or another of educational renewal is that work's previous tyranny over adulthood's time has been relaxed enough now to permit it. What we are seeing, in part, is an extension of the historic movement in industrialized society, however halting the pace, to accommodate the cumulative social and psychological needs of individuals caught in the gears of change. That history includes Bismarck's invention of the first social security system; the reforms precipitated by Lord Beveridge's comprehensive social insurance plan; the economics of Lord Keynes; the ebbing of the Social Darwinism of William Graham Sumner; the position secured by unions with passage of the Wagner Act; and such landmark legislation as the Social Security Act, the Employment Act of 1946, and the Manpower Development and Training Act of 1962.

But there is a perhaps more pragmatic consideration here. Another reason a lot of these people are taking these adult education and training courses is that they feel they have to, as part of their effort to keep up with their own jobs, or to qualify for new ones as technological change makes their previous skills obsolete.

Our employment and unemployment measurements provide no count of the workers affected by change or any insight into how they adjust to it, or don't. Technological change is still assumed to increase the *total* work available. but it means, inevitably, the constant displacement of particular workers on particular jobs. Increased productivity will mean losses of *certain* jobs in the industry involved, and there are other losses in industries that technology simply wipes out.

The Bureau of Labor Statistics found that from 1947 to 1957, although total manufacturing employment rose by 6 percent, there were declines in particular employments affecting 1,113,000 production workers. Increasing labor productivity accounted for 883,000 of these job losses; decreased production accounted for 230,000. From 1953 to 1959, when manufacturing employment *declined* by about 6 percent, the losses of particular jobs totaled some 1,540,000.[15]

While historically the United States has enjoyed favorable trade balances and net increases in employment as a result of international commerce, the situation became less favorable in the 1960s. Estimates of the effect of this one kind of change have not been very reliable, particularly because they are usually advanced in the heat of controversy. What is commonly stated as "the loss of employment," but which to be accurate should be expressed as "disappearing job opportunities," is estimated to have amounted to about 900,000 jobs between 1966 and 1973, this being the number of jobs that would have existed had not certain competitive products been imported. The impact has registered primarily in slower job *growth,* but there was clearly a significant *decline* during this period in textile, shoe, apparel, and automobile manufacturing, causing actual job loss. This number greatly exceeded the total of 43,000 who received adjustment assistance as displaced workers under the terms of the United States Trade Expansion Act of 1962.[16] There are no available figures on the number of people who lose their jobs as the result of the approximately 10,000 or so business failures that occur in this country each year.[17]

Another aspect of the retraining need that receives too little attention is that in 1973 some 6.3 million disabled persons were still able to work regularly but could not do the same work they had been doing prior to their disabilities. Among them, 2.6 million were unemployed or out of the labor force; most of them, though qualified for rehabilitation services, centered on occupational training, were beyond the reach of the existing Vocational Rehabilitation Program.[18]

Some idea of the magnitude of change at the workplace can be caught from the figures on the movement of workers from one major occupational grouping to another. According to Census data, one out of five workers moved from one *major* occupation group to another in the period between 1965 and 1970.[19] But this report grossly understates what is involved here, because it does not include any changes made *within* the large groupings. For example, a change within the category of professionals, from social worker to teacher, goes unrecorded. So too does a change from tool-and-die maker to carpenter, since both occupations are classified under craftsmen. Some further analysis of this data, and the making of several assumptions that cannot be confirmed but are conservative, lead to the conclusion that about 1.3 million people in this country move each year from one major occupational area to another under circumstances requiring significant retraining or education in order to make this change.[20]

The Department of Labor estimates that a twenty-year-old man can now expect that over the course of his working lifetime he will make between six and seven job changes.[21] Most of these moves will *not* involve a change in occupation. There are other data, from the Bureau of the Census, that suggest that this same man will—on the average—make one or two shifts (the figure comes out at 1.7) in major occupational grouping, one of which will require further education or training.[22]

These are boring figures. They are the dreary details, though, of the critical truth that there is an imperative necessity today for training and educational opportunity during the adult years just to let the individual keep up with change that works to the society's advantage, but for which it is unfair—and unnecessary—to make particular individuals pay the price.

To the extent that the job-opportunity structure equates better wages with higher skills, adult education and training can be one of the best—and cheapest—ways to fight poverty. As it is, about 2.3 million adults in this country earn less than a poverty income, though working full-time for a full year.[23] Beyond this, there are the much larger numbers who need, or want, to change jobs simply because their present jobs lead noplace. One study examined some 7 million jobs in eleven representative industries and found that over 2 million of them had no progression opportunities in the employing company.[24]

There is another implication in the accumulating evidence that many people feel the need to be better equipped for the jobs they already have. One study shows that one out of every five workers feels underqualified for his or her present job. To judge from this same study, others both want to move up and realize that they need to improve their abilities if they expect to do so.[25]

Most of the change described here has been viewed from the standpoint of forced job shifting or of reentry into the labor force. This is an obviously limited, and therefore limiting, perspective. For many of us, the most important aspects of lifetime change result from other forces than the pressures and stresses of a churning economy. Once we lift our sights to accommodate this reality, the present structure of lifetime educational opportunity in this country emerges clearly as not only inadequate but primitive. For, besides help in adjusting to a changing job "market" or in getting around blocked avenues of job progression or in making the jobs they've got more gratifying, we need the kind of help that will enable us to make the most of the *positive* changes in our lives—most notably the availability of increased leisure time in our middle and later years. The time has come to enlarge the perspective of the present adult education system in the United States to take in this larger horizon.

According to conventional wisdom, youth is the appropriate time for instilling in civilization's contemporary representatives all that is worth knowing from the storehouse of knowledge accumulated by representatives past. This premise needs to be reexamined. The broader knowledge base the society desires to impart, and may require for its survival, has been loaded so much on the youth years— one year of learning after another—that for many young persons education becomes a chore of life, a mean obligation more than the grand opportunity. In consequence, more and more people are concluding that a spacing out of education should be available to the young who are, in their own current terminology, being "spaced out" by overdoses and that "stop-out" privileges should be offered along the way. But it is equally important that consideration be given to adulthood's stifling monotonies. Stop-out opportunities for youth make sense. So does the option to "stop back in" later, as adults.

The assumption implicit in the defense of basic educational values has always been that living in the present is enhanced by an understanding of the wisdom of people who lived before or who have lived longer or have simply thought more. Putting all "utility coefficients" aside, this assumption is valid for people seventeen, thirty-five, or fifty-five, if it is valid at all. Whatever its hour, life is always precious. Advanced insight into why things are as they are, why individuals are as they are, what life offers and how it is secured, how other peoples and races live and think—such insight enlarges men's and women's humanity, including our capacity for cooperation. It doesn't diminish this ideal to recognize that the growth potential of the society and its economy seems encouragingly less finite in this context than it does if we concentrate our thinking solely on the earth's available physical resources and consider the exponential rate at which they are being consumed.

Education is not solely for the young, but a lifetime venture.

# 7.
# Work and Education:
# Coordinate Functions

The good sense in making education a lifetime venture—both to enrich the human experience and to increase the value of the economy's one boundless resource—warrants working toward the eventual establishment of a basic new right:

> Every adult ought to be entitled to five years of educational renewal opportunity—to be used at various points, depending on individual and societal circumstances.

This is a true horizon, within sight, though beyond present reach. Due regard both for its promise and for the barriers that must be crossed to approach it requires first a careful marking out of the various conditions for advance. By and large, these conditions can be grouped as follows:

First, present conventions about the provision of education and training—the institutional offering of it and the payment for it—will have to be significantly modified.

Second, comparable changes must be made in current customs and practices of the workplace, particularly as they involve training afforded there and as they affect worker mobility.

Third, we must be as concerned with the *process* of change as with the programs through which we hope to increase the opportunities for renewal.

## THE EVOLVING SCHOOL SYSTEM

We have some rethinking to do, generally about the adult condition, but most particularly about what actually will be required to
break up the time traps of education for youth, work for adults.
Here again the questions of who pays for what, and where the money
is to come from, have to be faced squarely. The kind of change that is
involved here doesn't just happen or come for free. Costs and values
will have to be carefully weighed.

### Honoring a Social Contract

A good place to start is where we thought we had already arrived—
with the notion that every American is entitled to twelve years of free
public education. A condition has been imposed on this right that
bears review: To get the twelve years of free schooling one must take
them when young. An adult wanting to return to a high school to pick
up where he or she left off would today be either prohibited by law—
or in any event actively discouraged—from doing so.

While some school systems sponsor programs enabling adults to
qualify for high school diplomas, a preliminary survey discloses a
variety of seriously restrictive practices, either by law or by custom.
Where persons over twenty-one are allowed by the state to return to
school, it is permissible under state law to charge tuition; sometimes
it's even mandatory, and Basic Educational Opportunity Grants are
not intended for adults wanting the equivalent of their first twelve
years of education. If the adults have a problem finding transportation, they probably won't be allowed to ride the school bus; the
insurance is usually written to cover liability for children only.

Some such restrictions are not readily apparent—for example,
those *de facto* in the Guaranteed Loans Programs. Under these
programs private institutions can make educational loans that will be
guaranteed by the federal government; in practice these institutions
may be giving the loans exclusively to young people, who have
parents who can be held liable. Careful study is needed to see how
much the time-trap premise had prevented those who didn't choose to
take their twelve years of free schooling in one dose during their
youth from getting what they are entitled to. While the technical legal
questions may not be clear, *the practical matter is that the right to
twelve years of free education is one of fixed duration.* What has been
considered an American social contract has time limits in the fine
print.

That this is of some importance to a considerable number of Americans can be seen in the following table, which shows how many persons, eighteen and over, have completed less than twelve years of schooling.

| Years of School Completed | Number |
| --- | --- |
| 1—3 | 2,654.000 |
| 4—5 | 3,782,000 |
| 6—7 | 7,504,000 |
| 8—9 | 20,735,000 |
| 10—11 | 16,605,000 |
| TOTAL | 51,280,000 |

Source: Bureau of Census, Series P20, No. 243.

More than 51 million adults (including, here, all those eighteen and over) have completed fewer than twelve years of schooling; about 14 million have less than an eighth-grade education. The figures for those who are in the labor force show some 13 million (age sixteen to sixty-four) with an eighth-grade education or less. And, statistics in terms of "years of school completed" leave out much of the story; a recent Public Health Service study indicates that some million twelve-to-seventeen-year-olds (most of whom are enrolled in school), many more males than females, and many more blacks than whites, cannot read at the beginning fourth-grade level.[1]

How many of these adults would take advantage of the opportunity, if it were afforded them, to pick up this elementary and secondary education they missed? This is exceedingly difficult to determine, for the answer has to take account not only of individual desire (which is influenced by prevailing assumptions regarding the availability or unavailability of the opportunity) but also of economic circumstance. Some have picked up "equivalent" education. The large majority of these 51 million have no significant interest in any further formal education. Nevertheless, the most careful possible evaluation of the available evidence shows that probably between 4 and 5 million, about 10 percent of the total, *would* make a serious effort at picking up what they missed, *if* the opportunity were available.*

---

*This is a National Manpower Institute estimate based on U.S. Office of Education data (in the Adult Participation Survey, made in 1972)[2] and the 1972 surveys conducted for the Gould Commission on Non-Traditional Studies.[3]

As things stand today, those over twenty find the public elementary and high schools closed to them, at least as a practical matter. They would be referred to the adult education department of the local public school system, if such a department exists. Only twenty-six states provide any funds at all for adult basic education, ranging from $42.4 million in California (FY 1974) down to $2,500 in Nebraska.[4] Local school districts are feeling a financial crunch that makes expansion of the adult education program seem an unaffordable luxury. What the answer to these people comes down to is: "For Children Only—Come Back Earlier."

This doesn't make sense, and in a lot of cases it isn't fair. There clearly is a potential here that should be developed, both in these individuals' interests and in those of the broader society. This means doing something further—to honor the spirit and the purpose of that social contract.

*Specifically, it should be adopted as national policy that a sum equivalent to the cost of up to four years of public education be made available for further education to any adult who has had less than twelve years of formal schooling.* The precise amount would depend, within the four-year limitation, on the number of years missed earlier. At current prices this would mean costs per individual ranging from $950 to $3800. The total bill would be large—in the multibillion dollar range, just how large depends on the number of takers— implying, in practical terms, a federally financed program.

The proposed arrangements would include a wide range of options—from enrolling in an institution of higher education, to a community college, or a private or public vocational school—and could include reimbursement to employers for training. Although the objective would not necessarily be the acquisition of a high school diploma, the General Educational Development Test could be used for those adults who want one.

Such a proposal has clear limitations, most obviously for the adult who needs income support to pursue education on a full-time basis. Indeed, part of the economics of full-time adult education is that its costs are higher than those of education in youth because of the greater foregone income. As it stands, the proposal would require extensive reliance on part-time schooling arrangements. There are, however, increasing opportunities for education that do not require full-time classroom attendance.

The costs will be high. But didn't we mean it when we decided that twelve years of education at public expense was a good public investment? Is it any less so if the individual makes part of his or her contribution (in time) at an older age rather than a younger? Who "owns" the unused portion of twelve years of free public education? And is it clear that the costs involved would exceed the returns? We should instead consider the almost certain prospect that every additional dollar so invested would return, with high dividends coming not only from larger contributions to the Gross National Product and to tax revenues but from reduced "welfare" and unemployment costs.

The central idea of *universal* adult education as a right has been much more fully—and persuasively—developed in the proposals of Alan Cartter, Gösta Rehn, Herbert Striner, Selma Mushkin, John Cotton, and Stephen Dresch,[5] all of whom have developed thoughtful plans for educational sabbaticals complete with financing schemes to bring them into being. But such complete plans cannot suddenly spring into being. Honoring the present contract is the place to start.

### Improving on Adversity

What has been suggested so far goes only to the "tuition" element of educational renewal. But what of the income-support factor that is so critical a part of any meaningful adult education concept? The doors to the future begin to open here with a recognition of the relationship of education and training not only to employment but in some respects even more directly to *un*employment.

Some relatively minor changes in the unemployment insurance system would permit a significant improvement in the use of involuntary idleness for education and training. In 1974 some 8 million persons drew unemployment benefits—a fourth of them for fifteen weeks or longer; 1.9 million exhausted their benefits without finding employment.[6] Had the rules been different, a large, but so far undetermined, number of these individuals would have used these periods for training and education of one kind or another.

Up until 1970 it had been a practice among the states to deny benefits to an unemployed person who enrolled in school on the grounds that that person was no longer "available for work"—a standard condition for eligibility. The federal law was amended in 1970, stipulating that "compensation shall not be denied to an individual for any week because he is in training with the approval of the State agency. . . ." While state laws have been changed, there has been no follow-up to see whether the spirit of the federal initiative is being carried out, whether individuals are being informed of the new

115

opportunities, and how many, in fact, are enrolling in training courses as a result. Over half the states have spelled out what "approved training" means, and a preliminary survey discloses three common restrictions on the scope of activity permitted:

- The training is usually limited to the type of skill training provided, for example, under the Manpower Development and Training Act (now the Comprehensive Employment and Training Act).
- The training must be for a job for which there is an identifiable demand.
- Other forms of education—especially those leading to diplomas—are usually not covered and are sometimes specifically prohibited.

Plainly, as a first step, claimants should be clearly and positively advised of their new rights, and reporting requirements on frequency of use instituted.

Federal or state action should also be initiated to broaden the terms and conditions of continuance of benefit payments during learning situations. It is entirely feasible for a counselor of the public Employment Service to determine whether a person with a particular set of skills, experience, and educational background is or is not likely to be reemployed, for that agency has available to it comprehensive information about the job situation. *It is proposed, therefore, that the unemployment insurance laws be amended to authorize and direct the Employment Service to determine, after a stipulated period of time (no more than five weeks) whether the "full employment" objective would be best served by permitting the unemployed individual to pursue—if the individual so chooses—a training or education program. Where the determination is positive the Employment Service should permit the continuation of benefit payments after enrollment and for the period of the individual's full entitlement.*

If this proposal were adopted, it would permit the combining of the support payments of unemployment insurance with the unused educational entitlements. It would be neither necessary nor desirable to keep the two sources of income earmarked—one for tuition, the other for income support. The two could be combined so as to provide the longest possible period of education or training, with the individual's making whatever distribution of benefits might be appropriate under the particular circumstances. During periods in which unemployment insurance benefits were extended under state or federal law, the extension would also cover education or training. A precedent for this kind of arrangement already exists in Massachusetts, which now extends benefits for eighteen weeks to a person attending "an industrial retraining course." Similar benefits are available under the Trade Expansion Act of 1962 to persons who have lost their jobs due to imports. The Act authorizes income support for a specified number of weeks, with provisions for extending this support up to twenty-six additional weeks if an education or training program is being pursued.

A number of specific details would have to be worked out in legislation and administrative practice. Questions will arise as to the effect of such arrangements on employer funding of unemployment insurance payments. More liberal use of these funds for educational purposes might argue for a government contribution to the unemployment trust fund. It would enlarge this retraining and education prospect if insurance benefits were increased. The June 1975 amendments to the emergency unemployment benefits program require new responsibilities on the part of the applicant to enroll in training programs, without requiring concomitant steps to ensure that the training opportunities are available.

The provision of this additional financial support for retraining would benefit those most vulnerable to shifts resulting from job dislocation, especially that caused by new technology. In the longer run, it would raise the educational and skill level of this segment of the labor force and contribute thereby to the strength of the economy.

There is, though, an infinitely larger and more significant dimension of this relationship between education and economic circumstances. Educational renewal opportunity should be available at all times; there are in the healthiest overall economy always large numbers of *individuals* having to make adjustments. Beyond this, however, as is pointed up by the economic state of affairs in 1975, there are alternating periods of expansion and contraction, and it makes sense to recognize this in administering adult training and education policies.

Recession is a time when a sizable percentage of the nation's work force is idled. It is a time when millions of people suffer both a loss of income *and* a loss of that feeling of adequacy and identity associated with holding a job. It is a time when tens of billions of dollars are paid out in *additional* Unemployment Insurance and Supplemental Unemployment Benefits negotiated through collective bargaining, food stamps, and welfare. This expenditure largely assumes that the recipients will be doing nothing but looking or waiting for work.

117

It is a time when people who *have* skills—foremen, technicians—are available to teach others, and when the equipment of many businesses is underutilized and can be used for on-the-job instruction. While not necessarily a result of recession, ours is also a time, and will be for many years, when there are teachers and professors who are available to teach those not needed at the work stations.

Recession plainly is a time of national crisis. But it is also a time when the cost of educational renewal is at its lowest, when income support programs are already paying out money, and when whatever additional government expenditure is necessary is entering the economy when it is most needed. These propositions have been well recognized in Sweden and put into practice in the form of a countercyclical education and training policy.

The concentration of education effort in recession periods has been the subject of intensive work by the Organization for Economic Co-operation and Development, and an integral part of the Active Manpower Policy that has been urged upon member countries. After a team of experts visited six member countries and a meeting was held to examine the results, this conclusion was announced (in 1972):

Variations in the number of persons occupied by training . . . should as much as possible counterbalance variations in employment proper and thus help otherwise unemployed persons to utilize their involuntary leisure in a useful way: Such an expansion of adult training during a slack period would also pave the way for a new expansion by increasing the available number of workers with skills in short supply.[8]

No such view of education training has yet become part of American policy, although the idea is being generated. An early 1975 editorial in the *New York Times* may be prophetic:

Unemployment now threatens to be severe and long-lasting, and it should be attacked by programs both to support and train the young and the unskilled and to meet important social needs. . . .[9]

It is proper to ask: Training and education for what? When jobs are in short supply what are people to be trained and educated *for?* The questions themselves reflect an assumption about the character and purpose of retraining programs for the unemployed. The sound approach has been thought to be to give fairly short-term training in a specific job skill for which there was "reasonable expectation of employment" upon finishing that training. That is sound, and what is proposed here is not an abandonment of it, but a moving beyond it.

*First,* there *are* jobs open even in recessions, and training for them is appropriate.

*Second,* offerings that require *longer* periods of education-training permit preparation for more highly skilled work. A year or so in such preparation is likely to see the end of ordinary recessions, and the longer time spent on a greater skill will increase the odds of using it.*

*Third,* a greater emphasis can be placed on creating more occupational flexibility for the *rest of a career* through development of second—and even third—job skills.

*Fourth,* there can be a conscious use of the "down time" of recessions to permit people to *shift* careers. Better it be done when the economy is not hard pressed for workers, than when it is booming and labor is in short supply.

*Fifth,* a conscious use of the down time to finish educations—a year to get a high school diploma or a degree from a community college—will mean long-term and sometimes immediate gains in future adaptability to economic change.

The converse of what has been said is that incentives for employed people to leave work for extended educational renewal will be much less in periods of serious shortage of workers. This may mean the working out of variable financial incentives to encourage educational renewal when the economy can most easily spare workers. The concept of educational renewal fits the business cycle, and the business cycle fits it.

## SETTING HIGHER SIGHTS

There are significant efforts under way to extend new forms of postsecondary educaton to adults who left the traditional schooling sequence at some point or other.

The College-Level Examination Program (CLEP) provides high school graduates, whether from last year's class or from a number of years ago, with a means for demonstrating their educational competence in an increasing number of subjects and enables them to get course credit for those subjects in which they have demonstrated competence. In colleges where open admission is practiced, candidates with CLEP-awarded credits are often required to show neither a high school diploma nor its external equivalent, the General Educational Development Test. The CLEP program reflects the

---

*All usual qualifications, of course, apply about care in looking at the trends as to which occupations are growing and which not.

complex links that are developing between secondary and higher education. It constitutes a working example of the fact that educational institutions can adapt themselves to changing situations and that the time-honored method of progress through school need not be sacred. There *are* alternatives.

Adult education programs have operated for many years on the periphery of higher education, positioned more to be influenced by than to influence the core of broader educational practice. There is a good possibility, now, that this balance will shift. Such efforts as the New York State Regent's Degree Program, the University Without Walls, "Minnesota Metropolitan," and the Empire State College operate relatively free of the encumbrances of traditional higher education. New clients are being served and new means of educational delivery are being experimented with. For example, "mentors" are being used rather than teachers, greater reliance is placed on the student to design and implement his or her own education program, and attempts are being made to use both established and new technology as instructional equipment. New means of both assessment and credentialing are being tried out.

Of particular note is the work of CAEL, the Cooperative Assessment of Experiential Learning program, a joint project of the Educational Testing Service and a group of colleges and universities, with initial funding from the Carnegie Corporation. The effort here is to develop a variety of means of assessing experience to see how much of it could be translated into academic credit. This project promises to create the links necessary for a smooth transition from work back to education.

Increasingly, as links between employment and higher education are strengthened, and as more and more specialized degrees are developed corresponding to various professional-occupational roles in society, a college degree is coming to certify possession not so much of a common educational experience but of a certain specific body of knowledge. Once this occurs, new forms of education delivery become possible. Large nonresidential universities are logical consequences of this perspective. Open universities providing "external degrees" are another. Patricia Cross in *Beyond the Open Door* contrasts the very separate assumptions behind credentialing practices that probably will coexist in America in the 1970s: Internal degree programs certify "the pathways regardless of the final level of accomplishment, external degree programs certify the level of accomplishment regardless of the pathway."[10]

## THE EVOLVING WORK SYSTEM

### Learning in the Workplace

It is a serious bias of most inquiry into education-work policy that it takes too little account of either the fact or the potential of education in the workplace. For a technologically based society, the United States has relied to an extraordinary degree upon informal, noninstitutionalized skill acquisition. A survey in 1963 showed that about half the workers in the United States between twenty-two and sixty-four, including two out of five "managers and officials" and two out of three "operatives," had no formal occupational training. Surprisingly, 46 percent of craftsmen and foremen reported no formal training.[11] A similar picture emerges from a Bureau of Labor Statistics survey of organized training in metal working, telephone communications, and electric utilities. In these industries more than half of all plants, and two thirds of small plants, provide employees with no formal training.[12] Another survey, of plants located in Cleveland, disclosed that only 12.5 percent give formal training on a regular and extensive basis. In that survey many firms said they give training only when forced to do so by shortages of workers and then drop it as soon as possible.[13]

One apparent reason for such limitations on training is the prospect that the worker acquiring it will then take it someplace else. Gary Becker, in his pioneering study of investment in "human capital,"[14] makes a distinction between training specific to the job and general training applicable to the jobs of other firms. He concludes that the employer is not motivated to provide general training, which may be used in a competitor's plant, unless compensated for it; but Becker's suggestion of lower wages during training presents serious complications.

Little systematic thought has been given in this country to encouraging private employers to sponsor training. A Task Force on Occupational Training in Industry has recommended federal reimbursement for training expenses. The reimbursement, however, would be limited to people with special handicaps and to special situations—when there are shortages of workers for critical occupations, for example.[15] Several European countries have enacted programs to stimulate employer-provided training.[16] In this country government assistance has been almost entirely confined to programs for the disadvantaged, such as Job Opportunities in the Business Sector (JOBS).

121

Both the needs of the individual and those of the economic system require that there be some solution to a situation in which the economics of competition seem to work against any single employer providing training for fear that it will become a benefit to competitors. Exhorting employers is not likely to be very productive in the absence of any valid cost-benefit analysis. We know very little about how much *is* spent on training for skills, and even less about the impact of an increase in that investment, on either upward occupational mobility for the individual or efficiency for the firm. We know virtually nothing about the kinds of inducements required to change the situation.

Any comments about a shortage of formal training in industry would be incomplete without reference to tuition-refund programs, whereby employers reimburse workers for job-relevant training and education taken at the worker's initiative. The increasing availability of these programs constitutes an encouraging base.

*Only a large-scale inquiry into industry practices and employer as well as employee needs will reveal the scope and nature of the possibilities here. Such an inquiry should be undertaken, probably most effectively through a combination of public and private agency resources, along lines suggested below.*

### Worker Mobility

Not only educational renewal but the whole work prospect is significantly affected by whatever may be, in the common phrase, the degree of "worker mobility in the job market." Those individuals who are able to change their occupations or to move from one employer or from one part of the country to another are obviously better able to adapt to changing economic circumstances and improve their earnings and working conditions. In general, such mobility decreases with the individual's age, dropping to a point in the United States where only four out of every hundred workers make material job changes between ages fifty-five and sixty-four.[17]

Possibilities for increasing worker mobility deserve more attention. Even with the highest of motives one hesitates to tamper with seniority, recognizing its critical importance. Still, some kind of reciprocity arrangements could be *added to* the traditional seniority concept to mitigate its restraining effect on worker mobility. In certain industries, notably building and construction, such arrangements already exist.

Private pension plans where there is no vesting constitute another barrier to job change. A significant step toward enforced vesting has recently emerged from Congresss in the Employment Retirement Income Security Act of 1974. Further advances will be required, though, for under the best of circumstances recognized by the new law an employee acquires full vesting rights only after ten years' service to the same employer.[18]

In many occupations licensing, ostensibly to protect the public, acts as an obstacle to free entry. A recent study discloses restrictive practices serious enough to call for legislative inquiry.[19] Often, licensing authority is delegated to members of the occupation, a practice not always compatible with promoting free access by qualified persons.* Certification procedures also exclude people who could do the work, or could learn to. The constraints here are often not a matter of law but of practice. Not only worker mobility, but broader work satisfaction will be enhanced by increasing the extent to which *competence* is the test for job entry. But this is bound to raise the issue of the balance between opportunity and security. Further thoughtful inquiry and experimentation will help. It will be worth finding out, when the results are available, what the effects have been of a 1969 legislative enactment in Japan that established a national skill testing and certification program, after which the number of occupations for which there are skill tests went from 78 to 200 by 1975.[21]

To assure maximum freedom in job choice, a competent public employment service is obviously critical. Repeated attempts to reinvigorate the job placement process of the public Employment Service have resulted only in a decline of its effectiveness. Since 1963 nonagricultural placements have gone down by 37.4 percent during a period when nonagricultural employment rose by 35.3 percent.[22]

### Flexible Work Time

How much the work experience is affected by the tradition of eight hours a day, five days a week, has been given too little consideration in this country. The practice bears a direct relationship to the possibilities of enlarged educational renewal opportunity. Recent experiments with flexible patterns of working time, with little or no change in total hours, are now stimulating increased discussion in both Europe and America. This is reflected, for example, in the

---

*More than 7 million people work in occupations for which licenses are required in some jurisdictions. About 500,000 workers are licensed in New York City according to a 1968 study.[20]

convening by the OECD of a conference in Paris in 1972 "to promote diversification and mobility in the regulation and allocation of time for work, study, and leisure, under the highest possible freedom of choice."[23] In Europe "flexitime" has come to mean considerable freedom for the worker to choose the portion of the day worked or what days are taken off.

A flexible arrangement has obvious benefits for workers. It allows time to schedule classes during what would normally be working hours, to schedule community activities, and even leisure, other than at night or on weekends. It presents difficulties for management, though, and the problems vary greatly with the industry. Potential benefits for both workers and employers are nevertheless possibly huge, and further study of this approach is clearly in order. A growing literature on measured effects of flexible schedules is now available.[24]

This particular matter is deliberately developed no further here. It is obviously the kind of subject that will profit much more from the collaborative undertakings of those who are involved than from any observations ventured from a distance.

It is appropriate to turn then to the kind of *process* that will test the validity—and provide the essential viability—of these program suggestions for melding the work and educational elements in the adult experience.

### PROCESS—A WORK INSTITUTE

Some of what has been proposed here clearly involves the prospect of legislation, at either the federal or state level, in some cases at both. This would be true, for example, with respect to removing the restrictions of time on the traditional twelve-year guarantee of free public education and also with respect to the suggested modifications in the unemployment insurance laws.

Whatever is done with respect to the expansion of adult education programs or the enlargement of community college programs will develop through established agencies of the educational system. To a considerable extent, too, there are already established processes and institutional structures within which a good deal of the probable future evolution of the workplace will occur. In-plant training is, by its nature, essentially a management function, except as particular situations have prompted the development of apprenticeship programs jointly administered by employer and union organizations. Procedures are also in place for dealing with the various elements affecting worker mobility (seniority and pension plans, for example, come within the traditional scope of collective bargaining) as well as for working out arrangements for flexitime.

Certain basic elements involved here warrant further consideration, however, of whether there is need for new forums for responsible and potentially effective consideration of the broader aspects of the work experience. A single question suggests the point: How long is it to be accepted as simply in the nature of things that the individual is to be tailored to fit the job—with so little thought of ever even looking at the other side of the possibilities?

That question cannot be raised lightly; it is too important. It is properly raised only with due regard to the importance of "efficiency" in the competitive production process and to the fact that the whole society benefits from that efficiency. And yet the improvement of the work experience is, conversely, important not just for individuals but also for the economy. As Jerome Rosow puts it: "Today the human side of enterprise looms as a critical factor in the accommodation of industry to a period of scarcity."[25]

Much of what has been written about changing jobs to make them more satisfying has concerned technique. The literature has dealt largely either with actual or proposed experiments to change production processes. Yet the key to the answers probably lies less in technique than in reaching consensus about goals: What importance do people attach to efforts to elevate job content? What do workers expect? What is an achievable demand? Superior managerial ability in the United States has shown itself able to adapt to great changes in markets, international competition, shifts in consumer taste, and changing availability of raw materials. Given agreement on goals, there can be equally effective attention to improving job content. There *is* such a thing as American "know-how."

While research and experimentation will be valuable, the decisive factor will be the chemistry of the situation—who provides the spark, what influences expectations, what degree of cooperation and collaboration exists between labor and management, how an atmosphere free of suspicion of others' motivations is created and maintained. A lingering fatalism about work—even some belief that it is not meant to be enjoyed—must also be put into the test tube. While no precise formula is going to be available, the proper elements can be identified in at least rough proportions. An agent is needed to foster cooperation and collaboration, reduce suspicion about motivations, and limit misunderstandings.

*There should be established what will be called here simply a Work Institute.* While some initial planning and organizational work would be required, sponsorship of such an Institute would necessarily be tripartite, with funds being contributed by employers, unions, and government. The Institute's policy-making body would draw its members, in an equal number from the public, employers, and union members, chaired by a public (but not government) member.

The beginning task of the Institute would be to provide a mechanism for interchange among the participants to search for some agreement on general goals and approaches—and define more decentralized structures for experimentation and implementation.

The agenda of such an Institute would necessarily be left open. This is important. The only listed item would be Work. What does work mean? Or rather, what *should* work mean?

Developing education and work as coordinate functions—and opening up the whole question of what they ought to be—implies getting into areas that must be explored carefully if they are to be ventured into at all. Such exploration can fruitfully proceed from consideration of these specific possibilities:

• That the cash value of the unused portion of "twelve years of free education" be available for a broad range of learning opportunities to those who did not receive that education in their youth.

• That the Unemployment Insurance system be adapted to provide income support for unemployed adults who pursue further education and training in order to make a job-market adjustment and extended for this purpose beyond normal duration periods.

• That additional educational options be developed for adults, with particular attention to open universities, certification based on competence examinations, credit for experience, and a broader community base for the expanding community colleges.

• That thorough inquiry be instituted into ways and means of creating workable incentives to increase employer investment in training.

• That in order to reduce the barriers to job mobility, consideration be given to more flexible seniority systems, to the fuller vesting of pensions, and to removing unnecessarily restrictive occupational licensing practices.

• That the principle of flexible work scheduling, especially for the purpose of dovetailing work with part-time educational opportunities, be applied as broadly as possible.

• That a tripartite Work Institute be established to work toward the development of a consensus about what work should mean and about how to give it larger meaning.

# 8.
# Three Revolutions

The case for weaving work and education more closely together rests essentially on the universal interest in life's fruitful pursuit. It has, nevertheless, a special bearing on three more particular interests that are currently the subject of unusual and strong national concern.

At an extraordinary moment of historical truth in the mid-1960s we declared our independence from previous bigotries about women and those we euphemistically call "minority groups." As we proceed now to make this new agreement in principle operative in practice, it becomes apparent that if we are to avoid the loss of at least a generation in this implementive process—*coordination* of changes in education and work policies as they affect these groups is absolutely necessary.

A third revolution—against the injustices we do ourselves as we get older—has not yet really begun but is an imminent prospect. The fallacies that "security" is life's ultimate door prize and that retirement is an unskilled occupation are becoming increasingly transparent. So, too, is the notion that if there are too many people in the work force the answer is to shelve everybody earlier. New thinking about the relationship between education and work may be as important with respect to the transition of older people from work, as work has traditionally been conceived of, as it is with respect to the transition of young people into it.

The consideration of an education-work policy must take into account its particular relevance to the completion of these two revolutions and the imminence of the third.

128

### HALF A NATION

The letter of the law that women are entitled to equal work, equal pay, equal education, is now clear.

So are the facts:

There are three men presently in the work force for every two women.[1]

• Among full-time, year-round workers, women's median earnings are only a little over half of what men's are ($6,335 in 1973 as against $11,186).[2] Men with high school diplomas earn about the same as women with college degrees.

• While as many girls as boys finish high school, women get only 43 percent of the college baccalaureate degrees, 36 percent of those for advanced college work, and 13 percent of the doctoral degrees.[3]

Of course the only work reflected in these figures is what has been traditionally conceived of as important to, and part of, the economy. It is possible to wonder a little ruefully whether the present concerns might be different if work or service performed in the home or in the community but on an unpaid basis had been included in the employment and Gross National Product figures. This is not a suggestion that women might then have stayed content longer with their present smaller pieces of life's recognized pie. The question is what the real pie is. If our thinking had been conditioned differently, our concern today might well be about how to equalize the opportunities of women and men alike for *all kinds* of human activity (with one notable biological exception). But "androgyny" lies virtually unnoticed and unknown in the dictionary's grave—or cradle.*

With respect to the unquestionably conditioned thinking about women's larger entry into the workplace, another set of preliminary adjustments must be made. The change is too often contemplated in the stereotype of a woman, subordinate to the breadwinning male head of the household, deciding to claim a job previously held by a man as a matter of virtually genetic entitlement. It isn't generally

---

*Not, however, entirely. There are, for example, new stirrings of interest among husbands and wives in the sharing of both academic appointments and the mixed chores and satisfactions of the hearthside. Androgyny is beginning to find its place in literature as well, for example in Mary P. Rowe's paper presented at the Centennial Convocation sponsored by the Association of M.I.T. Alumnae (June 2 and 3, 1973); entitled "Prospects and Patterns for Men and Women at Work: To Be Able Both to Love and to Work."

recognized that despite the unquestionable imbalance, women currently play a large part in the work force as conventionally defined; that there are already a very considerable number of working mothers; and that this is most characteristically a matter of economic necessity.

Twenty-two percent of American households, including 9 million children under eighteen, are "headed" by women—no husband present.[4] Sixty percent of women who work do so for compelling economic reasons; they are single, divorced, separated, widowed, or their husband earns less than $7,000 a year.[5]

Slightly over 45 percent of women sixteen and over work; they represent two out of five members of the labor force and from 1940 to 1970 accounted for about two-thirds of the increase in the working population. Participation of *mothers* in the labor force rose even faster, showing almost a fivefold increase—from 9 percent to 42 percent—in that thirty-year period.[6] For an increasing number of women the time out of the labor force for purposes of child rearing is becoming shorter; many stay in the labor force at least part-time while their children are young. One out of three women with preschool children is now in the labor force; 4½ million women with children under six are working.[7]

Women make up more than two thirds of all workers in apparel and other textile products manufacturing, general merchandising, and medical and other health services. They account for more than half of all employees in many other industries, including banking, insurance, eating and drinking places, and personal services.[8]

Such gross statistics obviously mix and mask both favorable and distressing circumstances. In any event, the stereotype of the American family in which a woman cooks, cleans, and takes care of the children—but doesn't "work"—is plainly an anachronism.

Presently, however, opportunities aren't meeting the demand. The male unemployment rate averaged 4.8 percent in 1974; for women it was 6.7 percent.[9] These figures leave out those women who have given up on the idea of getting a job, including particularly those who, though once employed, find the prospect of breaking back in to the labor force again overwhelmingly difficult and consequently do not try. The worst current oversupplies of labor are in fields in which women have traditionally specialized, such as teaching.[10]

It would be artificial to deal entirely separately with the adult and the earlier aspects of educational impacts on women's work opportunities. *The problems women encounter in the world of work warrant basic revision in the early socializing processes that shape for girls and boys alike their senses of identity and their ranges of life expectations.* These processes are pervasive. They operate in the media, in the family, in the early relationships among children as peers, and in educational institutions. The little girl from even a "liberated" household and a "progressive" school, when asked what she wants to be when she grows up, is likely to reply, "a nurse"—and her brother, "a doctor." So far, we only half sense the factors in this—and continue to look for others. A student at Douglass College, has noted the popularity among young girls of *Nancy Drew* and *Wonder Woman,* both successful adventurers into nontraditional roles. She is now exploring with her childhood girlfriends—an interesting "sample," not to be denigrated—what interaction there may be between the development of their self-images and their addiction to these fictional heroines.

New attention is being given the implications of the parallel downward slopes of girls' intelligence and achievement (and aspiration?) "scores." Preschool girls show up as well as boys on various intelligence and achievement tests; by high school and young adulthood, boys surpass them.[11] Why is this? How does whatever is involved here relate to the finding that men *apparently* achieve more success than women in at least some lines of work relying heavily on intellectual ability? How does it relate to the evidence, too, that at least until recently college women who, in their freshman and sophomore years were thinking of varied professional careers, were by their junior or senior year "conforming to reality" and thinking in terms of teaching and other traditional women's pursuits? We still know very little about the apparently constant pressures that convention has put on women's sense of accomplishment, autonomy, ambition, and self-esteem—often so subtle as to go unnoticed or so common as to appear normal in spite of the mischief they cause people of both sexes. Matina Horner, president of Radcliffe College, documents an extraordinary and palpable fear of success among academically talented women, apparently related to role uncertainty. If I am a woman, can I be successful? If I achieve, am I still womanly?[12]

*An essential part of the solution is in changes in the kind of education* and counseling provided girls. At a minimum, there is the need for in-service reeducation requirements for those in the high schools who counsel and advice girls—so that they can at least make clear the now broader horizons of women's opportunities. Older curricula and educational materials need revising to remove reflections of bias and to provide girls with new role models. This can be done by bringing into the schools—to talk with both boys and girls—women who have been successful in the changing education and work hierarchies, and by placing girls in experiential situations selected to cultivate a practical appreciation of the fact that their energies, skills, and abilities are needed and will be used across a wide band of activities.

The North Miami Beach Senior High School now offers courses on "Roles of Women," and "The Changing Roles of Women." A two-semester course on "Women (and Men) in Literature" is designed to "examine male and female roles as revealed historically through literature," and to "analyze modern conceptions of the male and female role" through consideration of such questions as, "Where do we get our notions of masculinity and femininity?" and "How significant is society in making us the kind of men and women we become?"

In Washington, D.C., a nonprofit employment counseling center—Wider Opportunities for Women—has launched Careers for Peers, a program designed to train high school girls in career information and resources, skill development, and job-hunting techniques. The girls receive school credits and paid fellowships, and serve as career counselors in their high schools; WOW cites "an obvious need to reach women at an age when career options are still open, sex-role stereotypes are not fixed, interest can be stimulated and explored, and new aspirations can be supported."[13]

The list of research and development projects sponsored by the National Institute of Education in fiscal year 1974, includes $50,000 to study sex bias and sex fairness in career-interest measurement; more than $450,000 for a variety of projects to examine present career guidance and counseling services for women and to develop improved counseling services for girls; more than $100,000 for curriculum projects to (1) review existing career education materials and programs with a view toward assessing their impact on girls' occupational aspirations and (2) develop special educational materials that will help young women understand the array of life choices open to them.

But efforts at improved counseling, curriculum development, and arranged work and service experiences will only increase frustrations *except as conventional institutional attitudes, practices, and policies, blocking women's routes to better jobs and new opportunities, are changed.*

The links to professional jobs, almost by definition, are through institutions of higher education. Yet at each educational level the percentage of women receiving the necessary credentialing degrees drops off. As has already been noted, women constitute 50.4 percent of high school and 43.1 percent of college graduates. But they receive only one out of seven or eight doctoral degrees. This last figure becomes even more instructive when it is broken down: women receive nearly 40 percent of all doctoral degrees in English, 35 percent of those in the arts and humanities, 20 percent in education, but only 2 percent in engineering, 10 percent in the physical sciences, 7 percent of the PhD's in mathematics, 11.6 percent in law, and 8.3 percent of those in medicine.[14]

A 1970 survey of graduate education led to this summary judgment:

Not excluding academic qualifications, sex is probably the most discriminatory factor applied in the decision whether to admit an applicant to graduate school.[15]

Title IX of the Education Amendments of 1972 now prohibits sex discrimination in the admission of students to institutions of higher education receiving federal financial assistance, and there is already dramatic evidence that the number of women being admitted is going up sharply.

If the routes to jobs through the higher education structure are more difficult for women, other routes may be even harder or totally closed.

Linkages between volunteer work and for-pay work remain extraordinarily underdeveloped, much to the disadvantage of women. So too are the routes from paraprofessional or technical positions (occupied disproportionately by women) to professional or scientific positions—for instance, nurse to doctor, laboratory technician to researcher, teacher's aide to teacher.

Participation of women in many union apprenticeship programs, especially in the craft areas, is increasing slightly but very slowly. There is, though, some progress. Better Jobs for Women, a Denver organization assisted by U.S. Labor Department funds, has been working to open the skilled trades to women. The very existence of this group reflects the necessity of taking extraordinary steps in order to encourage women to apply for positions in trades from which they have been barred in the past and equally to persuade unions and employers to fulfill the affirmative action requirements in federal contracts. Now in its second year, Better Jobs for Women has placed thirty-five women in skilled trades and craft training programs, among them the first woman plumber and the first telephone repairwoman in the country.[16]

Even where women are successful in gaining access to the programs, institutions, and experiences that are the usual qualifying requirements for entry or advancement in a particular occupational area, the result may still be in doubt. The case of the eleven women who completed all the necessary education and training to be ordained as Episcopal ministers of the church, only to find that their sex was the ultimate barrier after all, is generally taken to be the extreme and not the norm. This is not the view, however, of the Women's Equity Action League, which has filed a complaint against the *entire academic community,* arguing that educational institutions have failed to make reasonable attempts to find and hire qualified women for academic teaching positions.*

There is the case, too, of the Virginia woman who, after much perseverance, became, briefly, the nation's first firewoman—in spite of the outrage not so much of the firemen but of their wives, who were convinced that life around the firehouse was not conducive to proper co-existence between the sexes. More significantly, however, this case illuminates the broader problem that the organization and arrangement of so many work tasks have been designed on the presumption that only men are going to perform them. In many instances the physical aspects of the job *are* too difficult for women to perform successfully. Yet in many cases, too, relatively minor changes in design could bring the jobs within a woman's physical competence. With only a few adjustments in the job tasks performed and with some cooperation from their male colleagues, women are now working in the coal mines of Appalachia—to their own, their fellow workers', and their employers' satisfaction.

*The most critical adjustment in the circumstances of the workplace—essential to any truly meaningful equality of work opportunity—involves the development of adequate child-care services and facilities.* As long as the society proceeds on the assumption that child care is the woman's responsibility, arrangements are going to have to be made to facilitate child care if the mother is going to work. Whatever arrangements are made can, and should, recognize the logic that child rearing is a wholly shared responsibility. In many cases child care at the father's place of employment makes as much sense as providing it where the mother works.

---

*As required under Executive Order 11246 as amended by Order 11375 of October 10, 1968.

At present we suffer from a critical shortage of good child-care resources. There were 5.6 million children under six with working mothers in 1972. Only 905,000 of these were in licensed day-care facilities.[17] The remainder are provided for through some kind of informal arrangement that may or may not meet the need. A woman who cannot easily get good and reasonably priced child care cannot work herself out of poverty, cannot share equal job opportunity with men, and must forever weigh advancement in her career against commitment to the growth of her children.

The value of day care at the place of employment is well established. It makes transportation and family logistics easier, allows for contact during the day between parent and child, reduces the parents' anxiety about the child's welfare, provides opportunities for parent education in child care and for communication with teachers, and so on. There are now an increasing number of companies that provide day care for their employees' children. Other centers are run by unions, by hospitals, and by the federal government. The general reports are that the operation of such centers has been helpful in recruiting and retaining personnel, reducing absenteeism, improving motivation and productivity among workers, and improving community relations. There is increasing reason to support proposals that incentive tax credits be allowed employers who provide such services and workers who pay for them themselves—and that direct public subsidies for this purpose be increased.

The scheduling of work is another important factor. The conventional schedule—9 a.m. to 5 p.m., five days a week—precludes the participation of women in many work roles. There are obvious arguments for restructuring many types of work to better match the rhythms of human life. It is an important freedom to people, especially those with children, to work early or late, to get home in time to meet children coming home from school, to cooperate in running the day-care center, or to take a child to the doctor.

Attention is now being paid to arranging for employees to work varying amounts of time and on individual schedules, by days, by hours, or by parts of the year—and to the idea of contracting at the time of an employee's hiring for the amount of time to be worked within a period of a year or month, leaving it largely to the individual to set his or her own schedule. Where it is necessary in the nature of the work that schedules be planned in advance, employers can develop flexible work scheduling by the week or month.

*Serious consideration should be given to entitling women, by law,*

135

*to a year's educational renewal opportunity (either full-time, or part-time over a longer period) in connection with their moving—if they want to—from career motherhood to career something else.* This may not be the right form of the answer, and there isn't any way to anticipate how it would work out. But it is clear a large number of women, and probably about as many men, feel strongly that *some* kind of system must be developed to cover a transition situation that may well be as inadequately covered today as the transition from high school to whatever comes after.

Two cases are typical. In one of them, a comparatively early marriage and parenthood results in the husband's going on to finish college and perhaps law school and then to a job. The wife however does not go as far with her education as she meant to or at least does not get a chance to do what she thought she was preparing herself for. In the other case, the woman does go to work, enjoys it, and does well at it but then decides when children come along that she will give them all she has—"for a while." Five years after the break—or perhaps ten or fifteen—both women decide to go back and pick up on their earlier career courses, or possibly on entirely different ones. But they're rusty; so much has happened to so many career courses in the meantime. And they have zero seniority.

This doesn't make sense. We have recognized this in the case of military service. The GI Bill has been one of our proudest and most successful ideas; enabling a young man to do something else is the logical compensation for having taken him off his course to do something society demanded of him. And the veteran returns to work with "superseniority." Military service and motherhood are so different that the analogy leaves us uneasy. But motherhood seems to present an even stronger case for some arrangement of this sort. We have done *nothing* about it.

Now we probably will.

The discussion here has been, for the most part, as if the predicament of women were a problem in isolation. In fact it isn't. The life situations people of both sexes find themselves in are created by mutual interactions, mutual expectations and aspirations. Too often, men find themselves captives and prisoners of society's present education and work arrangements; women too often find themselves on the outside looking and hoping to get in.

The truly objective observer would probably find present sex stereotyping and lockstep patterns of living working against the interests of *both* women and men. We will probably move toward that view of it. For the present, though, the greatest impetus for change comes from a recognition of the inequity of the double standard we have established, even though we may eventually find a better single standard than men's present opportunities afford.

## STILL A DREAM?

In his preface to *Still a Dream,* Sar Levitan offers a terse description of what has happened:

No one familiar with the insufferable conditions of the not-so-distant past can doubt that blacks are much better off today than they were a decade ago. But improvement has been uneven and some dimensions may even have deteriorated.[18]

What is true for blacks is roughly true of all minority groups. To speak of "minority groups" in this particular context is to mean the 23.8 million blacks, 6.3 million Mexican Americans, 1.5 million Puerto Ricans, and .8 million American Indians who together make up about 16 percent of the total U.S. population. Although the situations of these various groups differ from each other with respect to educational and employment histories and opportunities, a summary of available information about blacks—by far the largest of them—will fairly indicate the difficulties common to them all.*

The prevalent situation is suggested in a single stark fact: the unemployment rate among blacks in this country runs consistently at just about twice the rate among whites. (In December 1974 it was 6.4 percent for whites, 12.8 percent for nonwhites.)[19] Pretty much this same difference shows up regardless of what age or sex grouping is looked at.

This double jeopardy rule has persisted despite anything done so far in the name of equal employment opportunity. The overall national unemployment rate was about the same (averaging 5.6 percent) in 1974 as it was in 1960. The unemployment rate among blacks was two times the rate among whites in 1960; in 1974 it was still two times as high.[20]

These unemployment figures *understate* the differences. A higher proportion of blacks than whites give up even trying to find work—at

---

*It should be noted that some of the governmental data that follow are developed on a basis that combines—in the traditional Bureau of Labor Statistics categories and terminology—"Negroes and other races" or "non-whites." Data above from the *Statistical Abstract of the United States, 1974.*

which point they drop out of the unemployment figures, being considered "outside the work force." Black *employment* is proportionately larger in lower-rated and therefore lower-paid jobs.

Another set of figures, covering educational attainment levels, needs to be set beside these unemployment figures. The most recent available figures here are for the year 1973. They show that the mean educational attainment among workers eighteen and over is 12 years for whites, but 10.8 years for blacks.[21] The fewer the years spent in school, the higher is the unemployment rate. To a slightly lesser extent, this is true among whites as well as blacks, but more blacks than whites have spent fewer years in school.

Would it help meet this situation, help reduce this disparity, if all adults were provided the educational renewal opportunities proposed in the preceding chapter? That's hard to tell. It might, for the terms of those proposals would extend opportunities in fact to proportionately more blacks than whites. The actual effect would depend, of course, on the *use* of the opportunities; and this might be harder for a larger proportion of blacks (with lower average incomes) than whites.

Another set of figures is relevant. It shows, for reasons that are not clear, an increasing tendency among black males (but not among whites) to drop out of the labor force during the prime work years:

*Percent in the Labor Force*

|  | 1953 | | 1973 | |
|---|---|---|---|---|
|  | *Whites* | Blacks | Whites | Blacks |
| Age 25 to 34 | 98 | 97 | 96 | 92 |
| Age 35 to 44 | 98 | 97 | 97 | 91 |

Source: Manpower Report of the President. 1974 Table A-4, pp. 257-58.

Is this because so many more jobs—especially those on career ladders—are now going only to people who have gone on from high school to take some postsecondary education, a group that includes (or did until very recently) proportionately more whites than blacks? In 1972 only 6.4 percent of all adult education enrollees were black.

It does appear that the start proposed in the preceding chapter, whereby those with less than twelve years of education would be recognized first, will be especially relevant to this group among whom a higher proportion did not finish high school. Similarly, any improvements on the quality-of-work front would especially benefit those blacks still concentrated in the less desirable jobs in the American economy. *A real affirmative action equal employment opportunity program must include, for those adults who have been discriminated against, at least the offer of a chance to acquire that education or training that they missed out on and that has now become the qualifying condition for so many more jobs.* It is important to bear this in mind, even though it is probably part of practical necessity to recognize that most of the essential educational and training component of equal employment opportunity will have to be added at the youth level.

The elements that have "conditioned" very young people's thinking, reviewed above with regard to the development of stereotypes about girls, are equally relevant here. Indeed they are so much the same that no point would be served in going over them again. Here, as there, *an effective education-work policy must start with improvement of the earliest opportunities to get it across to children—white as well as black—that some older people who should have known better have finally decided to correct a very bad mistake.* Unless this is done equal rights will again be put off for another generation.

This means seeing to it that the first schoolbook given a child—and every one after that—has had edited out of it every single reflection of that centuries-old mistake. It means going out of our way for a while to see to it that black and white youngsters alike see—live, in the classroom, where they can talk to them—people who can give validity to the fact that there *has* been a change.

The fact that high school counseling and guidance still tilt so strongly toward the college bound has a disproportionately adverse effect on blacks for two reasons. First, a lot more of them are still not going to college. Second, and more basic, in the absence of institutional arrangements, young people find their jobs largely through friends and relatives. Since the schools are not providing job placement services to any significant degree and the public Employment Service is not picking up the slack, the informal processes are all that are available. Inevitably the "friends-and-neighbors" network favors the whites who already have jobs.

The tying together of education and experience at the high school level, organized and facilitated by the proposed Community Councils, would create a vital access route to better jobs for black youth. Once a number of experience opportunities became available to the schools, formal public procedures could allocate them fairly.

The suggestion that public service employment opportunities be provided, if private employers cannot meet the entire need, would be especially meaningful when black teenage unemployment rates (now about 40 percent) are double those of white youth.

Although the high unemployment rates for black teenagers have been widely publicized, the *increasing* seriousness of the situation is not yet generally recognized. There is a history here of steady deterioration, a worsening of the situation of black youth relative to that of white:[22]

|  | *Black Teenage Unemployment Rate*<br>*as Multiple of White Rate* |
|---|---|
| 1955 | 1.5 times |
| 1960 | 1.8 times |
| 1965 | 2.0 times |
| 1970 | 2.2 times |
| 1973 | 2.4 times |

Another significant development—the marked drop over the past twenty years in black teenage *employment*—should be noted. In 1954, the first year these figures were kept, 38 percent of black teenagers were employed, compared with 43 percent for whites—a difference, but not a striking one. By 1973 the percent of black teenagers employed *fell* to 28 percent, while it *rose* for white youth to 49 percent.[23] Yet the enrollment of blacks in school in the teen years is not much below that of whites. It isn't clear what is causing these seemingly inconsistent developments. It *is* clear that meaningful equal employment opportunity depends on no less meaningful equal educational opportunity, and that *neither* of these has so far been achieved.

The barriers are slowly being torn down. But only affirmative action on both the educational and the employment fronts will produce the results that have been agreed to. Major surgery on these institutional relationships is essential to facilitate the integration of blacks into American economic society and at the same time to improve the quality of what it is they are integrated into.

## FOR WHICH THE REST WAS MADE

Robert Frost was sixty-seven when, more in resignation and acceptance than any bitterness, he rhymed his heresy: "Forgive, O

Lord, my little jokes on Thee/And I'll forgive Thy great big one on me."

Geriatrics may seem to be outside the realms of education and work, for "retirement" is defined in terms of finishing work, and schooling's "graduation" was decades earlier. Yet this, of course, is the point. For the superior possibility of constructive human improvement on the experience of aging may well be in extending, to the point at which the spirit as well as the flesh gets tired, the opportunities for both learning and contributing.

We have laid the essential *foundation* for whatever may be the structure of a policy regarding old age. Although important questions remain about the adequacy of the Social Security program, warranting continuing attention, the establishing of this security base represents a significant accomplishment.

The question now, however, is whether security is all there is to be to it. There is the additional important dimension of *opportunity*—the chance for people to engage in some form of *activity* as long as they have the stuff for it. The facts are that we are exacting, as the price for security, a tradeoff in curtailed opportunity.

This problem reaches back into the preretirement period, including the various forms and manifestations of prejudice—varying widely among different pursuits—against anybody past the "prime" of life, which is marked as earlier and earlier although all the evidence points the other way.

Here again, what is happening takes the form of a galaxy of attitudes that influence institutional arrangements: the mass of protective stereotypes that control hiring practices, promotions, retraining policies, and admissions to educational programs. "Older people lack flexibility." "They are slow and hard to get along with." "They cost more in terms of workmen's compensation and pensions." "They can't learn."

How valid are these assumptions?

The health and general physical fitness of old people may, certainly do eventually, affect their ability to participate productively in the labor force and to compete with younger workers. But there are many indications that aging affects ability to perform jobs at much more variable times—and on the whole much later—than is recognized in employers' practices, prejudices, and fears. Recent studies show that middle-aged and older workers perform as well in general as younger workers. For example, a survey of New York State employees found that workers over sixty-five performed "about equal to and sometimes noticeably better than younger workers."[24] Another recent survey reports: "In most jobs today, the physical demands are well below the capacities of most normal aging workers," and that "automation will undoubtedly make the physiological working capacity of the individual even less important."[25]

Moreover, the stereotype of the declining older worker may often be a *result* of the threat of retirement or unemployment. A University of Michigan study indicates that periods of anticipation of plant closing, unemployment, and probationary reemployment are correlated with significant changes in physical condition and psychological reactions—especially with respect to self-evaluation. While many symptoms returned to normal after the workers found new jobs, it is notable that estimates of self-esteem were much slower to come back. "The workers who had been terminated reacted as if their experiences had obliterated optimistic evaluations of their lives and their futures."[26] While these findings were among people in a wide age range, they unquestionably apply particularly to older people experiencing or approaching retirement.

Indicators much more sensitive than those presently available would be needed to correlate age with the performance of particular work tasks. It appears from the available evidence that the decrease in muscular strength that comes with age is relatively slight, while the factors that are more likely to affect job performance are decreasing perceptual and motor capacities. Indications are that older people become less able to perform or compete in jobs requiring special speed or fine visual discrimination, although even this would not hold true for everyone. The truth is, we don't know. There is little information, virtually none developed in the past twenty years, on meaningful correlations between older workers' abilities and the demands of their jobs.

Arbitrary discrimination against older workers is now prohibited by the Age Discrimination in Employment Act of 1967, passed after the Secretary of Labor filed a report to Congress noting that "the possibility of new *nonstatutory* means of dealing with such arbitrary discrimination has been explored. That area is barren."[27] But the knowledge that would permit greater certainty as to what individuals are able to do is insufficient and a limiting factor in achieving the full objectives of the law.

There is an increasingly fixed pattern of older workers' drift downward in their later years to lower-paying and less exacting jobs. Desirable occupations become closed to them, leaving them on jobs with lower pay scales and less attractive working conditions.

Disproportionately large numbers of older workers are in declining industries, occupations, and localities; they stay where they are because they know they are unlikely to get anything anyplace else. Those areas of employment that are rapidly contracting (mining, textiles, railroad transportation, farming) or slowly expanding (undertaking, pharmacy, small proprietorships) have proportions of older people two to two and a half times their relative size in the labor force.[28]

In 1970 the Social Security Administration found in a survey that one-half of the men interviewed who were subject to compulsory retirement said they did not want to stop working. The same survey found that these men realized a 60 percent cut in income after retirement.[29] The Age Discrimination in Employment Act of 1967 directed the Secretary of Labor to make a report on involuntary retirement. It has never been filed.[30]

As the actual cutoff date approaches, the employee may be brought into a "pre-retirement" planning program, but these programs are usually limited to discussion of insurance, pension plans, and company benefits. Few deal with the psychological aspects of adjusting to retirement or of retirement activities in general. A 1969 study of 100 firms showed that twelve companies had initiated "intensive-comprehensive" programs involving six to fifteen hours of individual or group counseling and discussion of benefits, planning, health, housing and leisure.[31] A Conference Board survey in 1974 reported that 88 percent (704) of 800 participating companies were offering preretirement assistance, and that 772 of the 800 companies now provide some form of *post*retirement assistance. This assistance, however, seems to be limited largely to sending pension checks and company publications, and to continuing medical and life insurance benefits in reduced amount. It was also found that relatively few companies take steps to find out how their retired employees are faring.[32]

To detail this pattern of what seems pettiness and even hypocrisy in the treatment of people as they get older is to realize that the real reason for most of this goes much deeper than we have so far been willing to recognize at all distinctly. It would be comparatively easy, if the people involved here were really wanted or considered needed, to correct the various elements in this situation: by *identifying and rooting out the discriminatory practices* the 1967 legislation prohibits, by *redesigning jobs* so as to permit older workers to do those parts of them they still can, by *providing training programs* that would facilitate their shifting to work using the capacities age has not diminished, and by *adjusting the compulsory retirement age* to gerontology's changing and on the whole benevolent realities.

The truth and the short of it, though, is that this is the area in which we are making our principal adjustments to the fact that there are more people in the work force today than are needed—at least within present perceptions and established notions. And a combination of developments—including advancing technology, an increase in women's participation in the traditional work force, a constriction of certain natural resources, and increasing human longevity—is contributing both to the pressures and to the seriousness of the consequences of our particular form of response. The old age security problem is much more fully under control today than is the old age opportunity problem.

Meeting this broader problem obviously reaches beyond even the widest conceivable perimeters of this Prospectus. Yet it is in this area that there will be a larger eventual necessity for developing a new architecture of education-work policy. For the answer to the need for opportunity as part of older age's experience will be found only in this devising of some form of "senior careers" for those who want them and in the arranging for the education and training some of these careers will require if they are to be meaningful—with the recognition that learning is itself one such type of career.

It would be a begining along these lines to at least start identifying those elements of activities of all kinds—infinitely varied in nature—that provide satisfaction to older people; and to undertake at the same time to inventory the currently unmet needs in the society that such people are qualified to fill.

Significant developments in this direction are already presaged by Title IX of the Older American Comprehensive Services Amendments of 1973 (P.L. 93-29), the reactivation of Operation Mainstream in 1974, and the establishment of the Senior AIDES Program by the National Council of Senior Citizens. But these prospects appear to be threatened seriously by both the elimination of the categorical approach to manpower programs and by the tightening up of federal financing of socioeconomic programs in general. New forms of initiative, more solidly rooted in the richer soil of local community concern, become increasingly imperative.

The prospect emerges of a reciprocally advantageous relationship between the older members of a community and the proposed Community Education-Work Councils. "Retirees," men and women alike, would bring to these Councils a wealth of experience that could be channeled to its obvious uses—in connection with the career guidance and counseling function, the development of local work and service and training opportunity inventories, the arranging of work or service experience opportunities, the development of Community Intern Programs, and so forth. The Council, on the other hand, would constitute an ideal forum and agency for developing and working out the details of what such an Operation Opportunity might come to mean as far as older people in the particular community were concerned—in the arrangement, for example, of adequate adult education programs, either through the schools or perhaps on a cooperative exchange basis among older people themselves.

There is another possible approach here: *to make a year's free public education available to everybody after he or she reaches age sixty, as an organized series of educational and training opportunities thoughtfully and carefully designed to meet this situation*—not just in the form of various and sundry "adult education" courses that the individual can put together from here and there.

The economics of such an arrangement would be less formidable than first reaction might suggest; indeed it isn't hard to think this possibility through in terms of a new (or at least substantially enlarged) "industry" that would pay its own way. And there is probably as much logic today for another year's public education after sixty as before twenty. The psychology of it is perhaps most important of all, for it could change materially people's attitudes about themselves and their place in society—at a time in life when there is particular question about whether there is a place at all.

In one way or another, the traditional concepts of both education and work—and of the relationship between them—must be adjusted to permit growth as long as there is life. It is Wittgenstein's reminder that "One does not live to experience death."

Women, "minorities," and all of us as we get older—three groups in three obviously very different situations. Pragmatically, though, they must be considered together, for they could constitute an effective coalition constituency for a meaningful education-work policy.

# III: The Prospect

"No sophistry is more demonstrable than that contained in the phrase the labor market, a phrase which grates upon the ear and offends the moral sense—for it seems to classify men with machinery, and fails to take into account human impulses and feeling, the heart and brain in their effect upon the energy and excellence of human industry.

"When Turner, the artist, was asked with what he mixed his colors, he growled out, "Brains"—and there is not a department of human labor, however mechanical, in which the enlistment of the brain, and with it the heart of the laborer, is not in a degree and way of its own of practical importance.

"Amid the elements of the cost of production, labor is ever present and essential, and consequently in the fierce and strenuous competition of the industrial world the true economy in labor, its quality as well as quantity, is the question of controlling importance."

Letter from the Honorable T.F. Bayard,
Secretary of State, to Jacob Schoenhof,
Esq., June 10, 1892.

LINDA: Willy Loman never made a lot of money. His name was never in the paper. He's not the finest character that ever lived. But he's a human being and a terrible thing is happening to him. So attention must be paid. He's not to be allowed to fall into his grave like an old dog. Attention must be finally paid to such a person.

*Death of a Salesman*

"All organizations increasingly will have to evaluate the human cost of loss and change. They are already called upon to think of the cost of their effects on the environment. The next step in the process of social evolution will be to weigh the costs of organizational influences on people.

148

# The Prospect

"It is predictable that, ultimately, psychological pollution precipitated by arbitrary and unthinking leadership action will become unacceptable and subject to compensation just as physical pollution and contamination are now subject to compensation. Weighing the impact of one's decisions on people's psychological attachments therefore becomes not merely a do-gooder interest. It is also an important matter of self-interest."

> "Easing the Pain of Personal Loss" by Harry Levinson, *Harvard Business Review*, September-October 1972.

"Job enrichment must eventually be translated into money—whether it is by reduced absenteeism, improved quality, greater productivity, reduced scrap, or whatever. If it does not get translated, then it will not become part of the existing system."

> "Twenty-Two Arguments Against Job Enrichment" by Robert H. Schappe, *Personnel Journal,* February 1974.

"That brings me to another point--money. If a person like me stays in teaching, people think there must be something wrong, because, certainly, I'd want something more lucrative or more prestigious like being a principal, a supervisor, or an associate superintendent if I could get it. That shows progress. If you stay in the classroom, there must be something wrong with you. You lack ambition or talent. We have no economic incentives like the administrators have. And a lot of good teachers are driven out of the classroom. When people yell about incompetence, they ought to look at what they're doing to foster incompetence."

> High school teacher, quoted in *Public Work, Public Workers* by Ralph J. Flynn (Washingon, D.C.: New Republic Book Co., 1975).

"When approximately one-quarter of our national adult population cannot qualify for a job that specifies a high-school education as a prerequisite, it's time something was done to correct the situation."

> Mayor Charles Puksta of Claremont, N.H., chairman of the National Advisory Committee on Adult Education, as quoted in Associated Press dispatch; February 5, 1975.

By the end of October, 14.7 million persons were receiving food stamps—up from the 12.4 million last year—at a cost to the Federal Government of at least $4.2 billion during the current fiscal year. . . . In Ingraham County, Michigan, where Michigan State University and Lansing Community College are located, nearly half of the 2,056 recipients of food stamps are students.

"There's little difference between getting food stamps and getting a scholarship, since the purpose of both is to lessen financial burden," said James Prome, a 21-year-old senior at Michigan State.

*New York Times,* January 2, 1975.

"Nobody really knows what the term unemployment means these days or is really sure of the size and makeup of the work force. Nobody ever seems to take the time to define just what these terms mean and nowhere do we get an inkling of where the numbers used to calculate these percentages come from or who actually compiles them. . . . To complete the compounding of the confusion, that cute little phrase, 'seasonally adjusted,' is usually added, and try as we might, we have yet to ever find an explanation of what that means or how it is applied."

Editorial, *The Hampshire Review,* "The Oldest Newspaper in West Virginia in the Oldest Town in West Virginia," January 29, 1975.

On Friday in Atlanta, 3,000 jobless persons broke down the doors of a hiring hall offering 225 public jobs.

Associated Press dispatch, January 12, 1975.

# In Brief

The preceding chapters have covered a broad range—from acquainting grade school children with what work and service mean to providing educational renewal opportunities for people approaching retirement. While these proposals have been advanced on their own merits, they have been put in the framework of two broader propositions: that the essential impetus for making these various changes will come only from the development of a *comprehensive* education-work policy; and that the larger development and use of the human resource is an increasingly critical element in the continued growth of the society and the economy.

It remains to consider two sets of questions regarding these broader propositions, involving, in general, their economics and their politics.

In its plainest form, the economic question behind a comprehensive education-work policy is "Who will pay for it?" How real is the prospect that fuller development of the human potential will be self-supporting? Will it contribute to economic growth? Chapter 9 is addressed to these questions.

The "political" question about a comprehensive policy, embodying so many different sets of self-interests, concerns how the initiative for such a policy is to be instituted. Granted the commonality of interests here—among youth trying to grope their way from classroom to employment, women trying to find some better purpose than being equal to men, blacks trying to recover from the fallout of bigotry, "gray panthers" seeking opportunity as well as security—who forms the working majority to enact the measures required? Who does what next in implementing a comprehensive education-work policy? Chapter 10 is a selective summarization of proposals made in the preceding chapters, putting them in a form designed to take account of the inevitably slow evolution of even the most imperative social change.

# 9.
# Unsurmountable Opportunity?

"Our problem," Walt Kelly had Pogo say, "is unsurmountable opportunity." This is about it. We know that there are limitless things to be done and that there is an equally boundless supply of human ingenuity and energy to do them. But, with the cartoonist's furry little philosopher, we encounter a profound bafflement about how to put this combination of demand and supply together.

It is posited in this Prospectus that at least a "key to that drawer in which lie other keys" is the recognition and fuller development of the human resource as a factor of limitless—and self-sustaining—societal and economic growth. But this is by no means either entirely clear or absolutely certain. Indeed, most of us react to this proposition with conditioned incredulity. It is the "self-sustaining" part of it we question. Who *produces* more, so that more time can be spent by more people getting more training and education? What is it then that these people are to *do* with more training and education that will be "productive" enough to continue the growth cycle? Who, in short, pays for an education-work policy?

These questions go beyond any fully established answers, But *parts* of the answers are clear, and it is important to mark out what we must do to get to the rest of them.

First, significant elements of an education-work policy involve simply the more effective use of monies already being spent for particular recognized purposes.

Second, increased education and training clearly contribute to economic growth in the traditional "Gross National Product" sense—but the evidence makes reliance on the "human capitalism" analysis at best uncertain.

Third, and most important, present and prospective national circumstance not only prompts but requires consideration of an alternative concept of growth—based on a different set of values—that includes the *prospect* of its being self-supporting economically. Investigation of this prospect requires the development of new measurements of circumstances, achievements, costs and benefits. These are the opportunities we have so far found "unsurmountable"—today they have an imperative new attraction.

## MORE RETURN ON THE DOLLAR

In a number of significant respects the pricing of an education-work policy is simply a matter of comparing the cost-effectiveness of the programs or procedures proposed with that of present practices. This would be true, for example, with respect to youth job placement. It is generally agreed that the millions of dollars a year spent—or at least in theory allocated—by the Federal-State Employment Service to finding jobs for young people are badly spent. A program of the kind suggested in Chapter 2 with respect to this function could be covered in large measure on a straight "transfer-of-costs" basis.

This would be equally true, as another illustration, of at least part of the proposal (in Chapter 7) for improving the unemployment insurance program to encourage the use of periods of unemployment for retraining and education.

Similarly, it can be strongly argued that a redirection of the federal employment and training program back more toward its earlier *training* emphasis, would serve to enlarge the skills and competences of those covered by the program—especially in a time of job scarcity.

Suppose there were a searching analysis made of the *present costs* of redundant employment—expensive to the employer and unsatisfying to the employee—as part of a broader inquiry into how the billions of dollars wasted on such employment could be made the basis for a retraining and reeducation program for the affected employees. The inquiry would unquestionably be opposed, at least at first and if the intent were left in doubt; but in cost terms the argument is pretty clear.

Work-study and cooperative education programs could be administered much more economically and effectively through the

Unsurmountable Opportunity?

clearing house office of a new Community-Work Council.*

Perhaps the largest potential economy of all lies simply in finding out what the comparative efficiencies are of the varous *present* education and training courses. It is entirely likely, indeed virtually certain, that the dollars-and-cents cost of every suggestion made in Part One would be less than the costs of the inefficiencies and outright wastes in the present system. This is not to imply that present educational expenditures are too high. They are not. They are too little. It is, however, to suggest emphatically that any sound consideration of the costs of weaving some larger "career" components into the educational system must necessarily include a comparable analysis of the cost-effectiveness of present efforts to achieve the same end.

A related, though slightly different, point is that some of the proposals made here would involve added costs for particular functions but nevertheless result in substantial *net* savings. This is clearest with respect to the improvement of the measurements and projections of manpower needs and career opportunities. For what would be pennies compared with the resultant savings, it would be possible to get reasonably reliable *local* data on an *occupation-by-occupation and industry-by-industry* basis—and to match these up with data on those preparing for various kinds of careers. Without this, the career planning now going on is a terribly expensive and often cruel delusion so far as a lot of young people are concerned. The price to industry of the skill shortages that exist, even under present conditions, continues to run needlessly high.

To a significant degree, therefore, the economics of an education-work policy involve simply the more efficient and effective use of monies already being spent to accomplish the same purposes.

## HUMAN CAPITALISM

The phrase is both enigmatic and jarring, and the pursuit of its meaning turns out to be a frustrating—but instructive—exercise. It is virtually self-evident on the one hand that the fuller development and

---

*No point is made here, though it arguably could be, that a number of the suggestions in this Prospectus—for example, those to do with the improvement of career guidance and counseling for high school and college students and the refinement of the career education idea—depend for their implementation on the use of volunteers and "representatives from the world of work." If the question is cost or cost-effectiveness, the analysis is incomplete if it leaves out the value of "volunteer" or "borrowed" services.

wiser use of the human resource contribute to economic growth; no one questions the larger productivity of an educated and trained work force or has any doubts about the importance of "universal free education" to the spectacular achievements of American capitalism. So there are the obvious elements here of an argument that still larger development and better informed use of people's capacities will in themselves strengthen the economy by increasing its growth in traditional Gross National Product terms.

Diligent inquiry, however, into the status of this concept leads, at most, to an ambivalence about its real significance, particularly as an element of policy formulation. On the one hand, there is scholarly analytical confirmation that education and training have been significant elements in the growth of the American economy and that they increase productivity. On the other, there is wide divergence of view about *how much* these contributions amount to, under what circumstances, and even about the feasibility of any reliable measurement of this. Yet, to the layman, at least some of this skepticism appears to reflect the economists' tendency to give too little attention to elements that are by their nature hard to fit into quantitative analysis. So there appears no alternative to fairly labored, and dubiously fruitful, pursuit of this concept for its obvious *possible* relevance to the economics of an education-work policy.

The base for the human capitalism concept has been the established economic theory that land, labor, and capital are the factors in explaining economic behavior, determining cost-benefit ratios, and measuring rates of return on investments. This theory recognizes that the fertility of land can be improved. It has, however, been slow to recognize improvement in the quality of labor as a factor in increasing the wealth of nations. The ambivalence with which this factor is typically regarded is perhaps caricatured by a 1957 textbook on economic theory, which prefaces its discussion of marginal productivity with the statement: "We shall assume that the labor is homogeneous in the sense that all workers are equally efficient. This is not an entirely reasonable assumption; but it will simplify our analysis greatly."[1]

In recent years, however, increasing recognition of the importance of the quality of labor has given considerable currency to the human capital theory.* It is now generally accepted that the level of workers'

---

*The analysis provided here of human capital theory and practice was aided by work performed by Alan LeBel of the Planning Research Corporation, and funded by the National Manpower Institute.

skills constitute a measurable factor in the growth of the GNP. Increases in productivity attributable to the development of higher skills are thus defined as the economic benefits of human capital; expenditures required for skill acquisition are the investment element of human-capital development.[2]

The human capital analyses proceed in the classical pattern, based on the familiar assumption that in a perfect competitive situation an employer seeking to maximize profits will expand operations until the marginal productivity revenue of an employee (the employee's marginal product multiplied by price) equals wages. The firm therefore will hire additional employees until the last person hired adds just as much as the equivalent cost in wages. The benefits and costs of increased workers' skills are then derived by using this same equation (wages equal market value of the product produced by the last worker hired). Within a time frame employers pay workers the value of their marginal product, and wages are believed to rise as education and training increase the quantity or quality of output per hour.*

Unfortunately, for present purposes, a good deal of the literature so far produced on this subject centers on the numerous theoretical and practical complications that arise in determining *how much* value is added by education or skill development, and then in translating that value into productivity and wage levels. It is essential, however, that these difficulties be clearly recognized, for important questions are involved.

The rate, for example, at which future benefits should be discounted to determine "present value" has to be chosen somewhat arbitrarily, and this choice greatly influences the outcome of the calculation. Earnings foregone while a person is receiving education are part of the "investment"—but obviously hard to determine. The "earnings" from education are normally computed in dollars and cents alone, but there is also the argument, made particularly by Gary Becker, that psychic returns should also be included. Related difficulties arise in taking into account the fact that, in general practice, investment decisions by individuals, employers, or others are not usually based solely on economic considerations. There are problems, too, in distinguishing between general and specific training. Special

---

*Where improved skill levels are permanent, revenues need not equal costs within a short time period, but they must equal each other over some particular time frame, usually calculated to include the number of time periods that represent the life of the skill acquired in terms of economic productivity.

importance attaches to dealing with the externalities associated with education—technological progress, possible reduction in delinquency, the attenuation of prejudices, and the undergirding of democracy and citizenship. Lester Thurow analyzed these methodological issues competently in his 1970 work on *Investment in Human Capital,*[3] and Ernst Stromsdorfer summarizes some eleven of them in his more recent analysis.[4]

Other types of problems are illustrated by Michael Borus' concern over the difficulty of finding adequate "control" groups.[5] Daniel Hamermesh points out that more research is required to determine the *means* by which education raises the productivity of labor, that past effort does not show whether positive rates of return are due to education's actually augmenting worker productivity or to the fact that it serves as a screening device.[6] Advocates of neither possibility, he suggests, have devised hypotheses to put the matter to a test. While Hamermesh raises problems *within the practice* of human capital theory, an analysis by Michael Piore questions the foundations of the theory itself.[7] Piore argues that it constrains the researchers to take the somewhat unrealistic views of the problem, to analyze them with inadequate techniques, and to reach conclusions that are not sufficiently encompassing for policy purposes. So a basic debate is joined over both theoretical correctness and relevance.

Giving due recognition, therefore, to the difficulties of the analyses involved, these studies yield impressive evidence of a substantial net return on investments in education—and persuasive confirmation that reliable methods can be developed to measure this return more accurately. The pioneering tabulation study by Glick and Miller,[8] using 1949 data, led to the general conclusion that an investment in a college education would yield $100,000 in a lifetime—compared to $24,000 if the same amount were invested in government bonds. That study was clearly handicapped by the limitations at the time on both data and methodology. Subsequent work by Dael Wolfle and Joseph Smith (1956)[9] and Miller (1965)[10] has advanced the methodology considerably.

A series of studies during the 1960s—by Gary Becker (1964), Gioria Hanoch (1965), W. Lee Hansen (1963), Shane J. Hunt (1963), and Daniel C. Rogers (1967)[11]—shows rates of return on investments in education running (with one small exception) between 6 and 22 percent. Some of these calculations are in terms of returns to the individual, others in terms of returns to the society as a whole.

In his 1974 study for the Brookings Institution, *Accounting for*

*United States Economic Growth, 1929-1969,* Edward F. Denison brought together the available information in this area. After a thorough analysis of the data, he concluded that the "fourth biggest source of long-term growth"—after advances in knowledge (technological, managerial, and organizational), amount of work done (the labor input, with the education component factored out), and capital—has been "the average amount of education held by workers employed in the business sector." He figured that this "increase in. . . skills and versatility was the source of 14 percent of the 1929-69 growth rate and 12 percent of the higher 1948-69 rate."[12] (Denison also notes two factors relevant to the point of this Prospectus: that confining his analysis to developments in the business sector results in a failure to reflect the even larger effect of increased education in government service and the teaching profession, and that there is a "definite countercyclical pattern" in the education input index.)

Attempts to measure the costs and benefits of training (as distinguished from education) have been given fresh impetus in connection with the evaluation of the effectiveness of programs established under the Manpower Development and Training Act of 1962. Here again, as with the education studies, serious problems of methodology have been encountered. Yet the results of these analyses have been unquestionably impressive; they show "internal social rates of return" from these training programs in a range (leaving out the extremes) of from 12 to 56 percent.[13]

The most recent—and most comprehensive—study to date followed people through Social Security records and found that the earnings of persons who received training in 1964 increased in 1965 to between 8 and 18 percent over what they would otherwise have been. Orley Ashenfelter, who conducted the study, concluded that while the training effects decline with time they still exist up to five years after training.[14]

It has also seemed worthwhile to survey what is presently available regarding the economic effects of programs undertaken in particular employment settings to improve the quality of work. In preparation for this Prospectus, James C. Taylor assembled a report* on eighty-one cases inolving the restructuring of work systems or job design.[15]

In few of these cases are the data completely adequate, and there is no way to arrange them for purposes of comparability. Some studies are reported in terms of percentage increases in productivity or

---

*"Work Experiments and Quality of Working Life; Economic and Human Results."

decreases in absenteeism, others only in more general terms. Under this circumstance, illustrative sample responses must be relied on:

- "Thirty-two and one-tenth percent increase in productivity."
- "Union members will demand new production procedures rather than assembly techniques after experience with both."
- "Production improvement ranged from 119 to 130 percent. Workers receive 19 percent to 30 percent more dollars."
- "From 1965-1969 grievances dropped from one per week to zero."
- "Twelve month results—no cost reduction but significant improvements in quality and attendance."
- "No significant change in productivity."
- "Satisfaction with supervisor improved."
- "Waste dropped to zero."

Although the results of this study permit no quantification, they point clearly and strongly to the conclusion that there *is* a tangible return—to the enterprise and the individual employees alike—from this kind of "human capital" investment.

This, then, is most of the "evidence" there is about the returns to society and the individual on investments in education, training, and improving certain aspects of the quality of work. A review of what we call, not entirely comfortably, human capitalism leads us out pretty much through the door by which we came in; it is clear that investment in people means returns in increased economic growth, but we don't know how much. A layman's license nevertheless permits, as an economist's professional standards would not, the conclusion that this return has been running someplace in the range between 15 and 25 percent—clearly large enough to encourage pursuit of the question of whether still fuller development and more enlightened use of the human resource would produce significantly larger growth, in traditional terms of that concept.

The case, then for further development of an education-work policy—in terms of its economic viability—is strengthened by the human capitalism analyses, but cannot advisedly be rested on this line of reasoning alone.

## NEW PERSPECTIVES AND MEASUREMENTS

The attempt to put education-work policy to the toughest-minded costs-benefits analysis possible demands at a minimum that we be clear about what we are after.

What costs are we talking about? Do we count only the money cost of doing something, or do we also figure in the cost—and loss—of not doing it?

And what benefits? Do they include *only* whatever increases the Gross National Product as it is presently computed, and raises the standard of living as that standard is today conceived of?

To what extent should we—and can we—take into account both costs and benefits that have no dollar signs on them but are nonetheless both clear and obviously important?

These general questions can be made a good deal more pointed by some others that are more specific and only in part rhetorical:

Are we reliably measuring the economic or the social costs of *whatever* is or isn't happening at the present gap between classrooms and whatever comes after by the dropout and youth unemployment rates to which we give such significance? Surely the bigger question—which we know virtually nothing about—is what happens *later* to those who are digits in these statistics?

What are the dollar costs to the society of supporting, over their lifetimes, the more than 1 million children under fifteen who are today not in school? And how do we measure the almost certain waste of that many human lives?

What *are* the costs of providing upper high school students with some work or service experience? If more of them had such experience would there be consequent savings to employers in lowered training costs and reduced turnover?

Various surveys show that millions of adult Americans (the figures range from 3 million to 18.5 million, depending on the standards used) cannot read the report cards their children bring home from school, or the help-wanted advertisements in the newspapers, or Medicaid applications, or the questions on the application for a driver's license. What does this mean in economic terms? In social terms? In personal terms?

What would be the costs of putting American work schedules on a flexible basis—taking account of *both* employer needs and employee interests? How would this compare with the dollar value—to the economy—of whatever people would do with their increased dominion over their time? And with whatever "psychic" value they would receive from it?

What would be both the economic effects and the effects on women's attitudes and lives if there were the same educational opportunities after maternity as there have been after military service?

How much would it affect both the economics and the psychology of geriatrics if Social Opportunity were developed as the complement to Social Security?

Two things must be recognized about both the basic economics and the realistic cost-effectiveness and analysis of a broader education-work policy:

First, these economics and this analysis rely only in preliminary part on the larger-return-on-the-dollar and the human capitalism approaches already summarized. Both approaches are important; a great deal more can be done about developing and using the human resource just by transferring present costs to more effective programs and by staying within the traditional concepts of reliance on that kind of growth which is reflected in the present computation of the Gross National Product.

But to confine thinking about an education-work policy within these perimeters would be to deny its real potential without exploring it. The infinitely larger prospect is that such a policy will lead to *new* growth potentials involving *different* values and individual and national achievements and that these additional growth possibilities will prove more fully self-sustaining than those based on the degree of exploitation of natural resources we have depended on in the past.

Second, however, the evaluation of this larger prospect—and indeed even any realistic cost-effectiveness analysis within more traditional concepts—depends entirely on our developing some *new measurements* of circumstances, of achievements, of growth, of costs, and of benefits.

There is no point in arguing further here what is necessarily, given the present yardsticks we use, the abstraction that fuller and better coordinated development and use of people's talents will result in a form of growth that will both conform more closely with our underlying ideals and pay its own way. This *is* the argument; and its advancement depends on indicating the degree to which we are presently relying on inadequate measurements, and the ways in which these measurements can as a practical matter be improved.

We don't realize the extent to which what we *do* in this country is affected by what we *measure*. Neither do we recognize the degree to which we keep our books largely in terms of *quantities,* with little regard for *qualities*. This is true only partly because the quantitative measurements are easier; it must be attributed also to the fact that our thinking about measurements has been set in quantitative terms.

The typical American reaction to the recommendations made above is that these concededly more important elements in what we are doing, especially those relating to the quality of life, "can't be measured." Yet to a considerable extent—enough to improve our efficiency greatly, and beyond that to affect substantially our standards of values—these things *can* be measured.

A review of present education and work policies and programs reveals serious deficiencies and gaps in the public record-keeping, particularly in the statistics that purport to document what happens during the transition period from school to work. While the human problems involved in this transition cry for attention, the data available—cast in aggregated abstractions about students, dropouts, and employed—force concentration instead on systemwide economic interests. Until school closing time on a given Friday afternoon, a boy or girl is considered a ward of society; then, suddenly, at eight o'clock the next Monday morning, he or she is "a unit of production," subject entirely to the whims or laws of the labor market. We recognize this as shocking error, yet fail to realize that it results in significant part from our keeping two separate sets of books, one for education and one for work—and from our measuring work in terms of employment and unemployment that will provide an *economic* indicator. Our system seeks to measure how the economy, rather than how the individual, is doing.

The figures on youth unemployment both exaggerate grossly and understate seriously the elements in this situation that are critical to doing anything about it except in terms of macroeconomic, countercyclical fiscal and monetary measures. Only in the fine print accompanying these reports—which the public rarely hears about— is it told that half the youth reported as unemployed are full-time students in school; or that the actual rate among large groups of these youth, especially minority group members and those in the center cities, is four or five times as high as the publicized overall average. To the extent that these youth unemployment rates are rising because of such things as increasing conjuncture of education and part-time teenage jobs, they actually become distorting factors in a total national unemployment rate even for purposes of measuring the health of the economy.

We will learn what this situation really is and what to do about it only as we find out some things the present economic indicators simply don't care about:

- How many of the unemployed youth (and are they boys or girls, black or white, or in a different group) are looking for how much of what kind of work and for what reasons (experience, economic necessity, pocket-money, boredom)?
- How many employed youth are doing how much of what kind of work? With what rewards? With what satisfactions—to themselves and to their employers? With what consequences?
- What are high school and college students doing in volunteer or service activities that provide equivalents of work experience but don't come under the work force heading?
- What are the differences on all these points as between sixteen-, seventeen-, eighteen-, and nineteen-year-olds, most of which isn't shown in the present record-keeping?
- What is the situation not just in the nation as a whole but in particular local communities where something can be *done* about whatever these figures show?

We have to know what *people* are doing and what *particular institutions* are doing—as well as just how the economy is doing.

Another critical element missing from the present measurements is any indication of the effect of the *sequence* of education and other experience in the lives of particular individuals. This can be supplied by what are called "longitudinal" studies. Only pioneering attempts have been made so far to find out what happens over the years to individuals who go through different educational and work experiences. Longitudinal studies are usually considered too expensive. But the price of *not* making them is that we have virtually no reliable basis for evaluating the influences of various elements in these experiences or the effectiveness of attempts to manage them.

Much useful longitudinal information about the movement of people from school to work and through their work life could be obtained at comparatively low cost by conducting retrospective surveys through the Current Population Survey and by exploiting the continuous work-history records of the Social Security System. Early job experiences would be much more objectively documented were the schools and the public Employment Service to institute a systematic follow-up of at least a representative sample of youth they place. The earlier examination (Chapter 1) of employer hiring practices with respect to youth strongly suggests: (1) the need for information as to what employer hiring policies toward people under twenty-one are; and (2) the companion need for studies showing how youth (with different degrees of education) actually perform on various jobs as compared with adults.

We simply do not know, today, except in quantitative terms of dubious reliability and relevance, what we are doing and what we are not doing with respect to the effective interrelation of education and work in the area where these two processes traditionally interlock, or are supposed to.

The monthly employment and unemployment statistics, particularly those that are widely publicized, are similarly sterile. They are limited, to begin with, to work done in the "labor market," saying nothing of what almost 60 million other people were doing, or not doing, at home or in the community during the survey week. The report is of bodies in place, or not in place, with little told of the growth potential or satisfaction in the work to either the employer or the worker.

The current employment and unemployment figures show very little of the actual degree of economic hardship involved. Yet it would be comparatively easy to develop composite indicators of work *and* earnings adequacy or inadequacy. Various ways of counting the total number of people with and without serious employment problems have been suggested. Generally, these consist of indices developed by adding to the unemployed some or all of such groups as the underemployed (using both those who want full-time work but can find only part-time work and those employed at poverty-level wages), and discouraged workers (people who have given up the search for work and are not counted as unemployed).* Such indices are potentially useful not only for measuring and studying the "universe of need—the number of people who have serious employment problems and for whom remedial programs need to be developed— but also as a way of distributing funds to localities in proportion to the need, although the data required to construct such indices are not yet generally available for particular localities.

The Comprehensive Employment and Training Act of 1973 requires the Secretary of Labor to "develop preliminary data for an annual statistical measure of labor-market-related hardship in the nation." Among the factors to be considered are "unemployment, labor force participation, involuntary part-time employment, and full-time employment at less than poverty wages." Thus, the need is clearly recognized, and action has been mandated.

---

*Examples of suggested methods: The Department of Labor's *A Sharper Look at Unemployment,* 1967; *Manpower Report of the President,* 1968; the articles in the *Monthly Labor Review* of October 1973, by Levitan and Taggart.

## The Prospect

There is much more that we need to find out, not just about those now considered as in the work force but about the broader human resource potential that is available. We haven't even started to ask the obvious questions:

- How many women, having raised their families or still in the process of raising them, want to do something else? What is it they want to do? Are they qualified by their education or previous experience—both matters of record—to do it? How much education are they willing to take? How much refresher education would they require? What value can be placed on their achieving what it is they have in mind?
- How many people currently reported as fully employed are in fact in sinecures created as refuges from advancing robots? How many of them could be retrained, at what cost, for other work?
- What is the waste in potential productivity and contribution from the compulsory retirement practices we are adopting?
- How many people are using which parts of their education, so far as this can be determined?
- What is happening in this country to leisure time—in terms of both its availability and its use?
- What firmer data base can be established, in terms of both productivity and worker satisfaction, for going forward with the current "quality of work" initiative?

It is perhaps an even more critical deficiency in the present national accounting system that we measure so inadequately what it is we are trying to do as a nation and to be as a people. Four times a year we get the report card on the Gross National Product. It, too, is lopsided—reporting all about quantity and nothing about quality, all about dollars and nothing about values, all about the system and nothing about people. If a dress is sold in a store, its price goes into the GNP; if one is made at home, that doesn't count. Collecting fees for pay at a hospital parking lot increases the GNP; a day spent in volunteer work at the hospital doesn't. This is a distorted mirror we hold up to see ourselves in. It makes it hard to be convincing about the value of increasing the development and use of the human resource. One wonders how our national priorities might start to change if we were advised regularly not just of the Gross National Product but of the Net National Achievement.

The situation would be different if there were better reasons than

166

tired convention for keeping these scales over our eyes. There aren't those better reasons. We pioneered in this country the development of a bank of "economic indicators" that have become models for the other countries of the world. In significant contrast, however, most of the nations with which we compare ourselves have now developed "social indicators" for which we have no significant parallel.

Japan inaugurated a Net National Welfare index in 1973, in addition to its measuring system paralleling our GNP index. Unpaid Service Produced for Households is figured in. Adjustments are made for Diseconomies Caused by Urbanization and The Diseconomies of Ecological Pollution. Cost of Pollution Prevention appears as a separate debit item in the computation of the Japanese NNW. The value of Leisure Time is included as a credit.

Two distinguished American economists, William Nordhaus and James Tobin have proposed a measurement of "Net Economic Welfare."[16] They would add to the GNP figure items for such things as housewives services and the value of expanded leisure time and subtract items like pollution and commuting as "non-material disamenities accruing as costs to the economy."

A first, tentative national report of *Social Indicators* appeared from the U.S. Office of Management and Budget in early 1974.[17] It covers eight areas—education, employment, and leisure and recreation among them. Under Education are items such as "Reading (and Science) Achievement by Selected Theme" and "Participation in Adult Education, by Sex, Race, Age, and Instructional Source"; under Employment. "Quality of Employment Life/Job Satisfaction"; under Leisure, "Daily Use of Time" (divided by sex and occupation, among leisure, personal and family care, work for pay, sleep). Although the introduction to this volume takes proper account of its limitations and of the infinitely larger prospects that available techniques could open up, we wait with some anxiety to see how far these potentials will have been developed in the anticipated 1976 *Social Indicators* report.

At a time when the critical constant has become an accelerating rate of change, it is even more essential that those measurements necessary for policy development be kept attuned to evolving social imperatives and public expectations.* In the absence of a dramatic

---

*A fuller treatment of this "measurements" point is in the separate monograph prepared in connection with the development of this Prospectus by W. Wirtz and H. Goldstein, *A Critical Look at the Measuring of Work* (Washington, D.C.: The National Manpower Institute, 1975).

crisis, the whole process of social change depends on the mass communication of quieter, cumulative crises.

While many separate steps will have to be taken to satisfy all the needs for new measurements, it would be a responsible first step to set up a Council of Social Advisors to parallel the Council of Economic Advisors, and a Joint Social Affairs Committee of the Congress to parallel the Joint Economic Committee. Such proposals have been before the Congress for some time,. and need to be acted upon. Perhaps the next step in this direction is suggested by the proposed Balanced Growth and Economic Planning Act of 1975. But "economic" planning is, in itself, no longer enough.

Only as these measurements are developed to consist with the human purpose will any valid cost-effectiveness analysis of education-work policy be possible. What is more important is that only then will we be in a position to evaluate fully the prospect for a different concept of growth and the extent to which it can be self-sustaining.

There are then, three factors in costing out an education-work policy, in determining its cost-effectiveness and whether it contributes to a self-sustaining concept of growth:

First, the case for a good many elements of such a policy—enough to get started on—is simply that they represent a better use of money already being spent.

Second, it is clear that some, although it is not clear how much, increased investment in human capital contributes to growth in the traditional Gross National Product terms.

Third, a fuller cost-benefit analysis—and the prospect of new growth potentials based on a fuller and better-coordinated development and use of people's capacities—depends on squaring our bookkeeping with our underlying ideals.

The limiting factors in surmounting our opportunities appear on analysis, however, not to be essentially economic. The more basic question, to which we now turn, concerns the political implementation of policies that experience commends and current circumstance makes increasingly imperative.

# 10.
# A Strategy for Change

*"How small, of all that human hearts endure—The part that kings and laws can either cause or cure."*

—Oliver Goldsmith

The logic of an education-work policy is compelling and the prospect full of promise. But the realization of this promise will be a formidable undertaking. It means realigning established institutional sovereignties. It involves readjusting life's conventional pattern, breaking down time traps that are constraining but have become insidiously familiar. It depends on reactivating the public's interest. None of this is going to happen just because it makes sense and is right. The rhetoric and logic won't count unless there is the clearest possible consideration of what strategy of change will permit the largest actual accomplishment.

The most difficult element in formulating such a strategy is that there is no readily identifiable spearhead for it, no single center of responsibility. The changes that need to be made can't be brought together in a single legislative proposal, even an omnibus bill. The undertaking will have to be at the local and state as well as federal level, engaging both public and private institutions, enlisting the society's membership as well as its leadership. The largest problem in developing this Prospectus has been not in suggesting the things that ought to happen but in facing the question of precisely who is to be expected to do exactly what *next*.

The realization of this difficulty, and that there is no easy way of meeting it, has prompted a considerable constraint in bringing conclusions and suggestions, for summary's purposes, into the form of actual recommendations. What this situation comes down to is that reliance is going to have to be placed on identifying those various beachheads of consensus that have already been established, so far as change in the area of education-work policy is concerned, and on then enlarging the beginnings. Only after that, and only as a larger force of momentum develops, can there be a realistic advocacy of bolder ventures.

Accordingly, the Prospectus proposals are summarized here in terms of a two-stage strategy.

Stage One includes those proposals that it appears reasonable to conclude can be effectuated, based on initiatives already undertaken, within the next two years; those in Stage Two being probably attainable within five years. The time frames are arbitrary, perhaps artificial. It is not suggested that the first stage will have to be completed before the second is entered.

Perhaps this staging approach is essentially a matter of internal discipline in the development of the ideas within this Prospectus. This approach is reflected, too, in the attempt—with respect to Stage One recommendations—to suggest the cost factors attendant on each proposal. It seems important, more broadly, to suggest what appear to be reasonable benchmarks of accomplishment. If the result of this approach turns out to be that the specific recommendations (especially for Stage One) seem to pale by comparison with the lofty purposes invoked in various earlier chapters, this is perhaps precisely the full justification for doing it this way. A constrained formulation of these recommendations is required by the fact that in the last ten or fifteen years of American history people in this country have wearied to the breaking point of proposals that assume too much and promise too much too soon.

*These things can be done:*

### STAGE ONE—ENLARGING PRESENT BEACHHEADS

**Proposal One: That there be established, in at least twenty-five cities, Community Education-Work Councils through which school officials, employers, members of labor unions, and members of the public engage collaboratively in developing and administering education-work programs; and that these pilot projects be carefully evaluated, over a five-year period and on a comparative basis, to determine their practicability and effectiveness.**

A design and various possible agendas for such Councils are suggested in Chapter 4. This recommendation is put first as a reflection of the emphasis throughout the Prospectus on the need for new *processes*—more than for any particular programs. It will be only as all of the constituencies affected by the interrelating of education and work are made active partners in this enterprise that the necessary programs will be devised and then carried out.

The cost of such Councils has been tentatively but carefully projected as averaging between $150,000 and $250,000 per community per year. The proposal contemplates the financing of these Councils through grants from private foundations, contributions from local community sources, and federal education and manpower training funds already appropriated.

**Proposal Two: That a comprehensive Occupational Outlook and Career Information reporting system be established, to provide (in both national and local terms): (A) "manpower need" projections over the next five years on an occupation-by-occupation and industry-by-industry basis, and (B) a complete report of the number of people engaged in all types of education and training leading (with a practical degree of specific expectation) toward various careers (Chapters 1, 2, ·3, 8, and 9).**

The clearest current consensus about the relationship between education and work is that no effective procedures have been established for matching training preparation with future occupational—or more general career—prospects. The interests involved are those of students, teachers and school administrators, and employers.

The underlying need here is for an adequate information base. In Chapter 9 specific recommendations are made for the development by federal statistical agencies of (1) complete, up-to-date surveys of the number of people engaged in all types of education and training activity, (2) more fully developed occupational and career outlook information, and (3) training experience surveys that will permit evaluation of the effectiveness of various kinds of education and training.

Lack of information does not constitute the most basic barrier to a smarter transition from school to work. Nevertheless, this is the place to start.

The costs involved, especially compared to prospective benefits, are relatively small. A fairly careful review of BLS and Census Bureau budgets indicates that an additional expenditure of between $3 and $5 million a year would permit expanding the present survey and reporting processes so as to provide an infinitely firmer base for relating education and training to career and occupational prospects.

**Proposal Three: That it be provided, as a total community undertaking, that all high school and college students receive at least five hours per year of career guidance and counseling from both professionally trained and work- or service-experienced counselors** (Chapters 1, 2, and 3).

Chapters 1 and 2 contain more detailed proposals for the critical guidance and counseling area, recognizing the *primary* responsibility here of the educational system and the essential importance of those with professional training. At the same time there is a critical need for some kind of community adjunct—including a volunteer corps of experience-based counselors—to complement the skills and services of professional counselors.

The costs here could be considerable. The best, but only rough, estimates of current national expenditures for guidance and counseling at the high school level put this figure in the $400 to $450 million a year range. A generous assumption would be that a fifth of this—something less than $100 million—goes for assistance in job selection. There is little immediate prospect for enlarging the present, so obviously inadequate, professional contingent. What can be done during the next two years will depend mainly on whatever increased use can be made of available community volunteers. The use of voluntary manpower does not eliminate the cost factor, and this recommendation is not meant to minimize it in any way. Still, an adequate guidance and counseling program seems expensive only when its virtually limitless potential for reducing human costs and losses is left out.

It may be that part of the sizable sum now being spent through the Federal-State Employment Service should be transferred to an improved career guidance and counseling system. In the longer run this could prove to be a better use of these funds.

**Proposal Four: That it be undertaken as a community responsibility to develop and administer programs to familiarize high school youth with work and service, including the provision of opportunity for at least 500 hours of work or service experience** (Chapters 1, 2, and 3).

While the value of experiential learning at the high school level is widely recognized, there is a persistent reluctance about trying to systematize arrangements for it. This reluctance stems in substantial measure from the mistaken assumption that this is to be another responsibility of the educational system alone. School authorities are simply not in a position to assume sole responsibility for seeing to it that every high school boy and girl gets work experience. Furthermore, when these authorities make tentative efforts in this direction, through school-arranged work-study programs and the like, the reaction of most employers is that they are being expected just to "come up with jobs" as manifestation of a corporate social consciousness. Labor unions, understandably fearful that the minimum wage laws may be compromised, are similarly negative.

The evidence suggests strongly that we now have all the makings of a complete experiential learning program if (1) service is recognized along with work as valuable experience; (2) the value is attached to the *general* elements of work and service experience rather than to special preparation for particular occupations or vocations; and (3) the program is developed and administered jointly by representatives of the educational community, the employment community, and the community at large, including students and parents—so that *all* the interests affected can be served. This will be essential in working out the answers to the questions this Proposal Four leaves open: Should the experience be optional or required? Should it be compensated, and if so on what basis? Should there be school credit for it? How are the values of experience at job *seeking* to be reflected? How are small employers to be brought into this system?

Preference in the proposal to broader aspects of the familiarization of youth with the nature of work and service contemplates, among other purposes, use of the suggested collaborative process (1) to bring men and women with other than academic work or service experience into high school classrooms, and (2) to provide elementary and secondary school teachers with opportunities for varied work and service experiences.

All that can be done about "costing" Proposal Four is to identify the elements involved, particularly two: the potential program costs if the work- or service-experience slots have to be subsidized, either privately or publicly, and the administrative costs.

There is obviously good use to be made in the community for 500 hours of the time (over a four-year period) of every youth of high school age who wants experience. A lot of this will be paid for, as it is now, on a value-received basis. If there are other situations in which the experience will be good but the pay bad (or nothing), there will probably be plenty of takers. It will have to be part of the rules that employers won't be permitted to exploit experiential learning situations to their competitive advantage, but they can't be expected to subsidize it.

Considerable administrative costs will be involved in developing experiential learning—and related work- and service-familiarization programs—as part of youth's secondary education. To underestimate these costs would be to discredit the importance of the purpose. There is an obvious function here for substantial volunteer staffs (in arranging the work and service experience assignments or opportunities), but this only changes the form of the cost. The employment community probably has enough self-interest in assigning its personnel to adjunctive roles in work-familiarization programs that adoption of this proposal would mean only minimal *added* cost factors.

**Proposal Five: That a considered break of one or two years in the formal educational sequence—taken between ages sixteen and twenty—be recognized and established as a standard optional phase of the youth experience, and that a comprehensive program of Community Internships and Work Apprenticeships be instituted at the local level (Chapters 3 and 4).**

The two elements of the proposal—the break and the internship-apprenticeship concept are complementary but not independent.

The specification of a *considered* break and for a one-or two-year period, not just the rest of the semester or an indefinite period is intended meaningfully. The proposal contemplates establishing procedures that will afford and strongly encourage *complete* career counseling and advice to the individual youth before the break option is exercised. This, however, does not imply that the decision to make this break would rest with anybody other than the student and his or her parents.

The proposal assumes the elimination of any institutional barriers to such breaks, especially with respect to the individual's subsequent reentry. The applicant for readmission will have a year or two of experience that he or she will be entitled to have recognized for whatever it may be reasonably considered, or found, to be worth. These people won't be dropouts or "stopouts" but people who have carried the work-study or cooperative education idea a step further. There will be interesting and critical credentialing questions here.

The suggestion of Community Internships and Work Apprenticeships is purposive but not prescriptive. It is increasingly questionable whether traditional private youth employment prospects will be sufficient to encourage the suggested break option. What emerges as a much more realistic prospect is that we will be able to identify— through the Community Education-Work Councils of Proposal One—significant work or service opportunities that could be developed along lines implied by internship and and apprenticeship. Internship suggests, at least generally, a service or paraprofessional function, possibly on a subsistence-wage basis. Apprenticeship at least connotes work experience—compensated on a learner-rate basis.

Properly, the thinking about this prospect will include a good many lessons from experience with military service, the Peace Corps, "national service," the service missions some churches have espoused and, perhaps most significantly, whatever is in the public employment concept that is relevant to the youth situation.

The potential cost elements in the internship and apprenticeship proposals are obviously very large. So are the potential benefits . . . and savings. But this cost factor probably warrants putting this part of the proposal (but not the "considered break") in Stage Two.

**Proposal Six: That a complete inventory be made of the extent and effect of laws, practices, and customs that constrain or otherwise influence people's movement between education and work (Chapter 2).**

This is a considerably broader matter than is generally realized. The laws to be inventoried range from those restricting child labor and requiring school attendance to those prohibiting the use of public funds to provide elementary or secondary education to people over a certain age. Some of these statutory constraints are obviously anachronistic; others present close policy questions. To extend the inquiry into the areas of employment practices and social attitudes is to encounter a variety of forces that, in their totality, affect very materially the movement, in both directions, between education and work.

By implication, the proposal advocates the removal of such constraints to the fullest practicable extent. This is most immediately important to the development of the experiential learning and internship/apprenticeship programs: problems or uncertainties, or both, arise in applying child labor laws, laws relating to hazardous

occupations, minimum wage laws, and school attendance requirements to experiential learning situations..

Restrictive employment practices will become more sharply defined
only as the studies are pursued, but some areas of concern can be
isolated: attitudes and assumptions about the capabilities of teenage
employees; gains and losses in worker mobility resulting from the
traditional five-day work week in contrast to flexitime; restrictions
inherent in seniority, pension plans, and credentialing procedures. It
is only with this kind of information that specific recommendations
can be made for removing the restrictions.

The costs involved here are only those of a comparatively broad-
scale research program, occupying perhaps ten people for most of a
year—say, $500,000 to $750,000.

**Proposal Seven: That a more effective capacity for integrating
education and work policy be developed at the national and state
levels.**

This proposal, included here as a logical parallel to the attention to
*local* governance in Proposal One, borders on piety. Interrelating
education and work is unquestionably complicated by the distribution of responsibilities for these two areas among a variety of agencies
in the state and federal governments. On this problem the clearest
consensus is probably that such "bureaucratic chaos" ought to be
cleared up. The jurisdictional problems are such, however that it is
almost impossible to say what can be reasonably expected to be done
within the two years of Stage One.

The provisions in a number of state constitutions providing for a
virtually total separatism of the educational system would probably
be eliminated or modified substantially if the public were given a clear
and open look at their effect. But this won't happen quickly.

Costs? These suggested reorganizations in governmental structures
would all lead to cost *reductions.*

**Proposal Eight: That a new Work Institute be established to
stimulate collaborative effort in the private sector to maximize work
satisfactions and meaning** (Chapters 5 and 7).

The conviction grows that new forms of attention to various aspects
of work will be to the advantage of both employees and employers.
The important element of consensus here has been somewhat
disrupted by questions and doubts that have arisen around the

quality of work rubric, particularly as it implies a change in institutional roles and threatens the balance of emphasis between increased worker satisfaction and increased productivity. These questions, however, serve to make the function of a "Work Institute"—to find the common ground of mutual and compatible interests—all the more important.

As conceived here, the proposed institute would develop broader public understanding of the work satisfaction issue complementary to the understanding sought by the National Manpower Institute in the education-work area. An anticipated $nnual budget for such an institute, which has already evoked the interest of several national foundations, would be in the $500,000 to $1 million range.

**Proposal Nine: That all state statutory and regulatory strictures on uses by adults of elementary and secondary public education facilities be removed or that alternative facilities be provided** (Chapter 6).

This proposal is important principally for its marking out, as part of Stage One, the important purpose of developing education-work policy in the interests of adults as well as of youth.

In more than half the states, present laws expressly limit the use of public elementary and secondary school funds to individuals who have not passed a certain age, usually eighteen or twenty-one. There are, however, more than 50 million adult Americans who have had less than twelve years of education, and the evidence is that a substantial number would like to pick up what they missed. These age limitations on grade and high school education should be removed. The social contract was not intended to limit to the young the right to a basic education.

This proposal will be misunderstood if the prospect of adults' picking up their basic education is seen as a return to traditional classrooms. The prospects for a comprehensive education work policy depend in larre measure on getting away from the strongly predominant notion of education as something afforded only in traditional settings. Experimentation with "open" universities and high schools is a preliminary step toward the exploration of a much broader area of possibilities. Cable television holds promise of infinite variety.

No cost estimate is possible here. The effect of removing the age restrictions in the present state laws will be limited by the constraining economic circumstances of most of those who would be

The Prospect

affected; they have to make a living. The potential prospective cost, however, may be of significant proportions.

**Proposal Ten: That the unemployment insurance laws and regulations be revised to permit and encourage the use of periods of unemployment for training and education, and that the "public employment" program and concept be revised to include a significant training and education element (Chapter 6).**

We are rapidly coming to realize that it is in the general as well as the individual interest that periods of joblessness be used so far as is practicable to develop additional skills and capacities. The Trade Expansion Act of 1962 provided an *extended* twenty-six weeks of unemployment benefits to individuals covered by that act who would use this period to train for new jobs. The 1970 Amendment to the general Unemployment Insurance Act provided for the first time that laid-off employees may continue to receive benefits (but only within the period of their regular entitlement) for the purpose of attending an "approved training course." There is reason today to apply the 1970 rule to "general education" as well as "training" courses—with the administrative safeguards already worked out. There would be widespread public support for going beyond this to give the 1962 Trade Expansion Act provision broader applicability, but the current strains on the unemployment insurance trust funds preclude this as a practical matter.

Attempts at costing out this proposal are frustrated by the fact that there are no available records on the use actually made of the privilege included in the 1970 unemployment insurance provisions; apparently there has not been much. Enlarging the option to include approved education as well as training courses probably would not increase costs significantly. It would be a mistake, however, to disregard the *potential* economic implications—going considerably beyond direct costs but including them—of a *major* expansion of adult education. (See Chapters 5 and 6.)

The June 1975 amendment to emergency unemployment benefits needs review; it tries to force people into training programs without making more training available.

The second part of the recommendation amounts only to an urging that attention now be given in this country to the European precedent—and the eminently sound reasons—for a countercyclical training and educational renewal policy. This would mean increasing

178

this program when the economy slackens and unemployment is high, with the consequences of workers being available for (and wanting) this activity (as an alternative to doing nothing), facilities for such retraining also being idle, and so forth. It would also mean cutting this program back, even below normal, in periods of increased economic activity and consequent larger labor needs. (See Chapters 5 and 6.)

It is only contemplated here that part of the funds that would otherwise go into "public employment" go instead—and to the same people—for public retraining and educational renewal.

**Proposal Eleven: That the present measurements of employment and unemployment (1) be expanded to provide adequate local as well as national data, (2) be revised to reflect more accurately the varying degrees of "economic hardship" incident to various types of situations, (3) be expanded to cover work and service performed in the home or community but not for pay, and (4) be reported and publicized in a manner differentiating fully between the various groups in the working population (Chapter 9)**

Present measurements of employment and unemployment are devised essentially for use as economic indicators. Both these figures and those covering much of the educational picture are body-count statistics, showing simply bodies in place or not in place. They say virtually nothing about the *causes* of whatever dislocation they disclose, and are equally noninstructive as to the *value* to either the individual or the system, of the education being received or the work performed. Both sets of measurements are artificially restricted: to education being received in classrooms and to work being performed in the competitive market. Both are gathered and publicized primarily on a national basis, concealing local or regional variances of significant degree. Finally, both are developed largely on a time-series basis, permitting a comparison of one year's situation with that of previous years but showing very little of what may be happening to individuals or groups of individuals as they move through the sequence of education and work experiences.

The humanization, or individualization, of these measurements is not so difficult as it sometimes is pictured. Specific suggestions for doing just this are outlined in Chapter 9 and set out in fuller detail in a separate monograph developed in connection with the preparaton of this volume.

## STAGE TWO—INTERIM OBJECTIVES

A disciplined first-things-first strategy of change still permits, indeed commends, trying to identify those initiatives that appear to offer the largest promise over a somewhat longer course. Four such initiatives appear reasonably identifiable: two involving propositions bearing directly on breaking up the education-work time traps, the other two relating more to the critical decision-making processes that will determine the eventual achievement of the still much broader purpose.

These four areas are appropriately marked out in terms of "propositions" rather than "proposals," to make clear that precisely how they are to be advanced must depend on what develops during Stage One. It has seemed pointless, for similar reasons, to attempt any comparably precise costing here; there is no present basis for even reasonable conjecture about the exact form these developments will take.

**Proposition A: That any adult who has not received twelve years of formal education be entitled to free public education, at whatever level is consistent with particular individual circumstance, to the extent of the number of years missed, but not to exceed four (Chapter 7).**

This would go beyond the effect of Proposal Nine—that age strictures on public education be eliminated—to the extent that an adult who satisfies experience equivalency requirements covering elementary and secondary education could use this additional entitlement for public postsecondary education or special training courses.

The benefits of this additional educational opportunity would accrue especially to those adults who have been particularly disadvantaged since they left school by the marked rise in the educational attainment level of the work force. It would have the special effect of making the civil rights revolution meaningful in the lives of older, as well as younger, members of minority groups. Equal employment opportunity has only limited effectiveness unless accompanied by equal educational opportunity, including this compensatory element.

It is properly noted here again, as in connection with Proposal Nine, that a good deal of this makeup education or training will probably be taken on a part-time basis and in forms not depending on traditional classroom attendance.

**Proposition B: That all adults be recognized as entitled to the equivalent of one year's Deferred Educational Opportunity (Chapters 6 and 7).**

This entitlement is conceived of as accruing after some stipulated period—perhaps five years—following the individual's leaving the regular education course, whether as a high school dropout or with a diploma, baccalaureate, or advanced degree.

The proposal is made with various work-related situations particularly in mind: for example, women shifting from career motherhood to something else as well; workers whose particular skills are no longer needed, or who simply want to do something different; people approaching retirement and looking for something more than security. But the proposition is in no way limited to work situations, differing significantly in this respect from the promotional-leave-of-absence statutes of Western Europe.

The proposal as made here contemplates, in effect, free tuition, to be used for courses of the individual's choosing. It does not include any additional support elements, falling considerably short in this respect of the sabbatical and the West German and French precedents. This exclusion obviously diminishes the significance of the proposal greatly, but this will advisedly be left for subsequent consideration. The tuition entitlement alone involves a potential cost or investment in the billions-of-dollars-a-year range, depending on how many individuals take advantage of the proposed opportunity.

These Propositions A and B, along with Proposal Nine, probably press the general idea of a lifetime continuum of educational opportunity about as far as a disciplined strategy warrants at the moment. They add, in effect, a thirteenth year to the twelve traditionally conceived of as so important for everybody that they should be made available at public expense. Taken in conjunction with Proposal Five, they break up the single education-work sequence idolatry, and they touch a little on the point of considering periods of slower economic activity and higher unemployment as particularly propitious times for increased educational and training activity. They obviously have only limited relation, however, to the broader prospects envisaged in the discussion in Chapter 9.

**Proposition C: That adequate measurements of the development and use of the human resource be made and published as part of a comprehensive set of social indicators, and that a Council of Social**

Advisors to the President and a Joint Social Affairs Committee of the Congress be established (Chapter 9).

This proposition is, in short, that there should be instruments for social planning comparable to those used for economic planning. The imbalance between these two functions requires correction if such purposes as the significant interrelating of education and work are to be served.

The "measurements" point is as vital as it is undramatic. No significant comprehensive education-work policy will develop so long as the Gross National Product retains its currency as national gospel and continues to be defined in the conventional terms of productivity. The common assumption is that national priorities are established first, that policies are then established to implement these priorities, and that achievement is determined by measurements calibrated to the priorities. It is at least as true thatpriorities as well as policies are determined by what bookkeeping system is set up.

The proposed Council (to the President) of Social Advisors and a Joint Congressional Committee on Social Affairs parallel, perhaps too patly, the present Economic Council and Joint Economic Committee. Only through the sharply focused attention of such agencies can we learn to understand the perimeters and parameters of growth based on the fuller development of the human resource. A proposal for the creation of such agencies has been before the Congress for most of ten years, receiving substantial support but never with effective concentration.

**Proposition D: That there be an increased effort to develop a process for drawing, at the local community level, on the American citizen's authentic desire to participate more fully and directly in the improvement of the human prospect.**

The suggestion in Proposal One for setting up something like Community Education-Work Councils proceeds from the identification of particular functional needs—to provide career counseling and guidance, develop work-study programs, etc.—that by their nature defy adequate handling by the established institutions alone and would be greatly advanced by broad community participation. A number of other elements in the interrelating of education and work generally present this same situation. This is equally true of a good many other areas in which older forms of special-interest organization and institutionalization no longer satisfy the demands of an increased interdependence among virtually all interests and interest groups.

The evidence appears in increasing volume now—polls, surveys, and analyses of various kinds—confirming (1) that people feel increasingly "left out" and that "what they think doesn't count," (2) that there has been an incriminating drop in the public's already dangerously low confidence in *all* established institutions, public and private alike, and (3) that a meaningful number of people are now ready to "get back in"—at least (4) if they can find some *new way* to do it.

This expressed affirmative intent meets no single standard of what is good and what isn't. It includes the intent of those who propose to meet school busing their own way instead of the courts,' and of those who consider themselves as individuals the appropriate censors of all children's schoolbooks. Yet this is a problem democracy has lived with for two hundred years—with no clearer answer than that people are more right than wrong when enough stand up to be counted.

It becomes, therefore, a counsel not of despair but of new hope that the American people have it in mind to draw again on the essential principle that originally cemented this society and has maintained it for two centuries. There *is* a renewed sense of concern. There *is* a renewed consciousness of community.

A committee or a council set up for a particular purpose—vocational guidance and counseling, or the development of experiential learning—probably wouldn't have much staying power. Yet the fuller use and development of the human resource, the development of a new meaning of growth based on the fuller use of the human resource as the limited supplies of natural resources dwindle, the breaking up of life's time traps, the highest and best use of the life experience—*these are* purposes that will inspire and sustain new adventures in responsible self-government, if they can be made into real prospects instead of just resounding rhetoric.

There is particular reason to think this can be done at the *community* level today more effectively than on some broader scale.

Making sense out of education and work offers superior opportunities for the memberships of local communities to participate in improving life's quality, for youth and adults alike.

The architects of change, considering what can be done within the next five years, will consider intently what new institutional forms will serve this purpose and harness this authentic American force.

So the single key to the development of an education-work policy may well be that enough people in enough local communities around the country assert enough willingness to get involved in a toughminded, practical way in again assuming responsibility for at least this one set of their affairs.

*And then . . .*

To look hopefully but hard beyond the next five years in the development of an education-work policy for America is to recognize that its future depends on a broader course of events. At the same time, what we do during the next five years can be a key element in the shaping of that future. Everything in this Prospectus for such a policy has been shaped to what appear to be the four critical elements in a return in this country to a Politics of Idealism.

First, the American people today are deeply skeptical about any grandiose representation. They have been oversold for too many years on too many grand initiatives. They have become incredulous about everything they are told and everybody who makes any new promise or proposal. The first demand on policy today is that it be totally *credible.*

This education-work policy—identified deliberately in a bland phrase, no acronym possible—has been set out, accordingly, in spare and disciplined terms of particulars that are clearly do-able, assuming only the most reasonable diligence.

Second, people are willing to consider only what they can be shown the results of and what they are satisfied they can pay for. The second demand on policy today is *fiscal responsibility.* This is the reason for emphasizing so strongly here the mundane and undramatic subject of measurements and evaluation. It is the reason, too, for identifying the importance of contributing through the fuller development and use of the human resource—which is what the coordination of education and work is all about—to the revitalization of the idea of growth unlimited for the nation.

Third, people in this country today want very much to start thinking again in terms of human values rather than just about a Gross National Product. The third demand on policy today is that we speak to the *quality of life.* An education-work policy *will* improve the prospect of a higher and better use of the life experience at the stage called youth but equally across its broader course. There *is* a human desire to break out of the time traps of youth for learning, midlife for earning, older age for obsolescence. Education and work *are* human values.

Finally, today, people in every American community and every walk of life feel left out—that they don't count. They want back into their own affairs. Representation, at least through the established channels, isn't enough. The fourth demand on policy today is that it provide the opportunity for *participation*.

This is the reason for pressing so strongly here for the development of citizen involvement processes, particularly at the local community level. An education-work policy offers superior opportunity to return to a Politics of Idealism in America.

# Notes

## CHAPTER 1

1. Data showing the breakdown of the youth unemployment rate derived from the *Manpower Report of the President,* 1974, Table A-6, p. 260, and *Employment of School Age Youth, October 1973* (Summary: Special Labor Force Report, Bureau of Labor Statistics, April 1974).

2. Between 1950 and 1970 the number of people in the age group five through twenty-four increased from 46,943,000 to 77,142,000 (a rise of 64 percent). Source: *Current Population Reports,* P-25, No.s. 310, 470, and 476 (Bureau of the Census).

3. This commitment is reflected in the public's willingness to spend an increasing proportion of the GNP on public education. In 1929-1930, total expenditures for education were $3.2 billion, and by 1970 they were $77.6 billion. Source: *Digest of Educational Statistics, 1971* (National Center for Educational Statistics), Table 25, p. 21.

4. U.S. Office of Education, *Biennial Survey of Education in the United States; Statistics of State School Systems: Organization, Staff, Pupils and Finances* (OE Series 20020, 1953-1954 through 1969-1970).

5. More than a million of these children out of school are under fifteen; over three-quarters of a million are between seven and thirteen. Children's Defense Fund, *Children Out of School in America* (CDF, 1746 Cambridge St., Cambridge, Mass.)

6. Adapted from the *Digest of Educational Statistics, 1972,* (National Center for Educational Statistics), p. 8.

7. Jerald G. Bachman, Swazer Green, and Ilona D. Wirtanen, *Youth in Transition,* Volume III, "Dropping Out—Problem or Symptom?" (Ann

Arbor: Survey Research Center, Institute for Social Research, University of Michigan, 1971).

8. *Current Population Reports,* Series P-23, "The Social and Economic Status of the Black Population in the United States, 1971" (Bureau of the Census), p. 79. There was a 19 percent increase in the number of black students in college in 1974-1975 over 1973-1974. Jack Magarrell, "Black Enrollment Rising Again," *Chronicle of Higher Education,* March 17, 1975, p. 1.

9. Data and quotation are from *Employment of High School Graduates and Dropouts, October 1972,* "The High School Class of 1972" (Special Labor Force Report 155, Bureau of Labor Statistics, 1973), p. 29.

10. In the official survey, whoever is home (often the mother) speaks for the labor force status of the whole family. In the less official but validated longitudinal survey sponsored by the Labor Department (the Parnes Survey) the youth themselves are asked about their employment status. The statistical variations are significant. In the Parnes Survey of October 1967, the labor force participation rate of white males enrolled in school, aged sixteen and seventeen, was 58 percent, compared to 42 percent in the regular survey, and 56 percent for eighteen- and nineteen-year-olds compared with 41 percent. The differences were even greater for black males: among sixteen-to-seventeen-year olds, 50 percent in the Parnes Survey compared with 35 percent in the regular survey, with comparable figures of 61 percent and 31 percent for eighteen-to-nineteen-year-olds. See Herbert Parnes, *et al., Career Thresholds, Volume 2,* (Manpower Research Monograph No. 16, U.S. Department of Labor, 1971).

The differences in the two sets of data are mostly accounted for among the employed, rather than the unemployed. Similar, but smaller, differences also exist for teenagers out of school. Possibly much of the difference is in reporting part-time work, thought to be more important—or better remembered—by the youth than the mother.

The greater labor force activity found by Parnes raises the question of whether there were differences in employment and unemployment rates also. Employment and unemployment varies from the Current Population Survey differently among different subgroups. For sixteen-to-nineteen-year-olds as a whole, the youth reported much higher employment than is recorded in the regular survey, leaving the overall unemployment rate the same for the Parnes and regular surveys.

11. *Manpower Report of the President,* 1971, Table B-6, p. 198.

12. Calculated from the *Manpower Report of the President,* 1971, pp. 203 and 209; and the *Manpower Report of the President,* 1973, Table A-2, p. 128, and A-7, p. 135.

13. *Employment of School Age Youth, October 1973, op. cit.*

14. Data on eighteen- and nineteen-year-old males are from a special tabulation by the Bureau of Labor Statistics. Data on twenty-five-to-forty-four-year-old males are from the 1972 *Current Population Reports* (Bureau of the Census).

Notes

15. The question of what difference a high school diploma makes was explored directly in the longitudinal study carried out by the Survey Research Center at Ann Arbor (Jerald G. Bachman, *et al., op. cit.*). The study involved a national panel of 2000 boys, starting in 1966, in the tenth grade at the time, and resurveyed every year. The Bachman report is consistent with another massive longitudinal survey, *Project Talent* (John C. Flanagan, *et al.,* American Institutes for Research and University of Pittsburgh, 1971).

We do know that years of school, and the certification that results, do make a difference in occupational success in later years, although it seems to be credentialing more than a result of any effect that staying in school longer has on cognitive ability. And, where staying in school longer helps in employment, it may come about because of the characteristics that lead the youth to stay in school, rather than schooling itself. This knowledge comes from the many studies reviewed by Christopher Jencks and his colleagues. However, for males a high school diploma seems to make little difference in the *teen* years. Female graduates seem to do better than their dropout counterparts, but females as a group have an occupational distribution heavily shaped by stereotyping and discrimination.

16. Thomas W. Gavett, *et al., Youth Unemployment and Minimum Wages* (Bureau of Labor Statistics, Bulletin 1657, 1970), p. 75.

17. Daniel Diamond and Hrach Bedrosian, *Industry Hiring Requirements and Employment of Disadvantaged Groups* (New York University School of Commerce, 1970).

18. Special tabulation prepared by the Bureau of Labor Statistics.

19. Denis F. Johnston, "Education of Workers to 1990," *Monthly Labor Review,* November 1973, p. 23.


## CHAPTER 2

1. The Bureau of Labor Statistics has published a set of four volumes of *Tomorrow's Manpower Needs: National Manpower Projections and a Guide to Their Use as a Tool in Developing State and Area Manpower Projections* (Bureau of Labor Statistics, Bulletin 1606).

2. In the school year 1953-1954, there were only 4800 persons providing guidance and counseling in elementary and secondary public schools; by 1969-1970, the number had jumped to over 46,000. Office of Education, *Biennial Survey of Education in the United States,* op. cit.

3. *Agenda for Action: A Report of the Guidance Advisory Council to the Board of Education of the City of New York* (New York: Academy for Educational Development, July 31, 1972); the ratio for San Diego is from *Agenda for Action's* "Survey of Large City Guidance Systems," p. 48.

4. Robert E. Campbell, *Vocational Guidance in Secondary Education: Results of a National Survey* (Columbus, Ohio: Center for Vocational and Technical Education, Ohio State University, 1968), Table 18, p. 33.

A survey done by Jacob Kaufman, which was more geographically limited (17 schools in Pennsylvania) than the Campbell survey, but more intense, disclosed that:

> The typical counselor observed in this study was involved 10 percent of the time in keeping records, 50 percent in conducting interviews, 8 percent in administering tests, 2 percent in handling disciplinary problems, 19 percent in communicating with teachers and 11 percent in other general activities.

Jacob Kaufman, *et al., The Role of the Secondary School in the Preparation of Youth for Employment* (University Park, Pennsylvania: Institute for Research on Human Resources, 1967), pp. 4-13.

5. Calculated from Table 18, Robert E. Campbell, *op. cit.*

6. The Bureau of Labor Statistics is currently developing a publication for junior high school students. "The junior occupational outlook handbook is tentatively entitled *Exploring the World of Work.* Written in a simple style, it will introduce young people to some of the basic information about the world of work and careers. It will succinctly introduce basic concepts about the changing nature of the economy and how jobs are created. Occupational clusters, the relation of occupations to school subjects and educational levels, and the connection between job characteristics and individual interests and abilities will be discussed broadly." *Occupational Outlook Quarterly,* Fall 1973, p. 31.

7. One example is a set of materials put together by the Bureau of Labor Statistics as a part of a ten-city pilot program to make labor market and guidance information available to youth in ghetto areas. Fifty different occupational outlook pamphlets have been developed for use in Employment Service offices, schools and Model Cities Agencies. *Occupational Outlook Quarterly,* Fall 1973, p. 31.

8. Data supplied by the Public Employment Service, Manpower Administration, U.S. Department of Labor.

9. Data from a survey titled: *Jobseeking Methods Used by American Workers,* to be published as a Bureau of Labor Statistics Bulletin.

### CHAPTER 3

1. John Dewey, *Democracy and Education* (New York: The Macmillan Company, 1961), p. 9.

2. E. Alden Dunham, *Colleges of the Forgotten Americans: A Profile of State Colleges and Regional Universities* (The Carnegie Commission on Higher Education, McGraw-Hill, 1969), p. 1.

3. Frank Newman, *et al., Report on Higher Education* (U.S. Department of Health, Education, and Welfare, Office of Education, 1971). The report was prepared by an independent task force funded by the Ford Foundation.

Notes

4. *Youth: Transition to Adulthood,* Report of the Panel on Youth of the President's Science Advisory Committee, James S. Coleman, Chairman (Office of Science and Technology, Executive Office of the President, June 1973).

5. Project description dated March 11, 1974, titled "A Study of Schooling U.S.A.," September 1, 1973-August 31, 1978. (Institute for Development of Educational Activities; Inc., an affiliate of the Charles F. Kettering Foundation).

6. George Tolley, "Higher Education and New Patterns of Learning and Work," July 1973, p. 1. (Mimeographed.)

7. Leland Medsker and Dale Tillery, *Breaking the Access Barriers* (New York: McGraw-Hill, 1972).

8. Interview with Kenneth Skaags, Specialist in Occupational Education, American Association of Community and Junior Colleges, April 1, 1974.

9. Edmund Gleazer, Jr., "What Now for the Community College?" *Community and Junior College Journal,* December-January, 1973 (Washington, D.C.: American Association of Community and Junior Colleges).

10. Alan Pifer, Speech at American Association of Community and Junior Colleges' Annual Convention, Washington, D.C., February 24, 1974, p. 13.

11. Medsker and Tillery, *op. cit.*

12. Adapted from "Summary Data Vocational Education Fiscal Year 1972" (Office of Education; Bureau of Adult, Vocational, and Technical Education, 1973).

13. *Ibid.*

14. Office of Economic Opportunity, *Federal Youth Programs: A Discussion Paper,* 1972, p. 40.

15. These figures were extrapolated from data on enrollments in cooperative education, work-study, NYC In-School, Federal Summer Employment Programs, Youth Conservation Corps and University Year for Action. A rough guess was made as to how many are involved in internship programs. Total number of enrollments in these "work experience" efforts was taken as a percentage of enrollments in high school (junior and senior years only). The freshman and sophomore high school enrollments were not included, because few programs are aimed at youth in this age range. Obviously the numbers and percentages represent very rough guesses.

16. Information from program brochures and interviews with program personnel by National Manpower Institute staff.

17. For evaluations of work experience programs see: Ernst W. Stromsdorfer and James S. Fackler, *An Economic and Institutional Analysis of the Cooperative Vocational Education Program in Dayton, Ohio* (Bloomington: Indiana University, March 1973); Systems Development Corporation, "Executive Summary of an Assessment of School-Supervised Work Education Programs" (USOE Contract #OEC-0-72-5024, March 1973); *Federal Youth Programs, op. cit.;* Systems Research, Inc., "Survey and Analysis of In-School NYC Programs" (July 1973); Ernst W. Stromsdorfer, *An Economic Analysis of the Work Experience and Career Exploration*

*Program (WECEP)* (Bloomington: Indiana University, July 1973); and Joint Economic Committee Report, "The Effectiveness of Manpower Training Programs."

18. Stephen K. Bailey, Francis V. Macy, and Donn F. Vickers, *Alternative Paths to the High School Diploma* (Syracuse, New York: Prepared for the Ford Foundation by the Policy Institute, Syracuse University Research Corporation, 1973), p. 131.

19. *Manpower and Vocational Education Weekly,* April 23, 1975, p. 2.

20. The Work Experience and Career Exploration Program (WECEP) allows jobs for youth under sixteen, serving primarily fourteen- and fifteen-year-old youth identified as dropout prone. The Colorado Youth Employment Opportunity Act is another early positive step toward loosening some of the restrictions of the Child Labor Laws. See Sylvia Weisbrodt, "Changes in State Labor Laws in 1971," *Monthly Labor Review,* January 1972, p. 37.

21. Ernst W. Stromsdorfer, *An Economic Analysis of the Work Experience and Career Exploration Program (WECEP), op. cit.*

22. Thomas W. Gavett, *et al., op. cit.,* pp. 69 and 72.

23. For a summary of the federal laws, see *A Guide to Child Labor Provisions of the Fair Labor Standards Act* (U.S. Department of Labor, Child Labor Bulletin No. 101, 1971). For state laws, see *State Child Labor Standards* (U.S. Department of Labor, Bureau of Labor Standards Bulletin 158 [Revised 1965]). For an historical summary, see *Child Labor Laws* (U.S. Department of Labor, Wage and Labor Standards Administration Bulletin. No. 312), reprinted from *Growth of Labor Law in the United States* (U.S. Department of Labor, 1967).

24. Thomas W. Gavett, *et al., op. cit.*


### CHAPTER 4

1. See the address of Luvern L. Cunningham, Co-director of the Detroit Education Task Force, *Third Parties as Problem Solvers,* presented to the David W. Minar Memorial Conference on "Problems in the Politics and Governance of the Learning Community," Northwestern University, November 1, 1974.

2. Cyril O. Houle, *The External Degree* (San Francisco: Jossey-Bass, 1973), p. 74.

3. A. Harvey Belitsky, *Private Vocational Schools and Their Students* (Cambridge, Mass.: Shenkman Publishing Company, Inc., 1969), p. 9.


### CHAPTER 5

1. T. C. Cochran and W. Miller, *Age of Enterprise, A Social History of Industrial America* (New York: Harper, 1961).

2. Walter S. Neff, "Work and Human History," in *The Social Dimensions*

*of Work,* ed. Clifton D. Bryant (Garden City, N.J.: Prentice-Hall, Inc., 1972), pp. 36-52.

3. Source: Data for 1948 computed from the 1964 *Manpower Report of the President,* Table A-7, p. 199. Data for 1973 are from the 1974 *Manpower Report of the President,* Table A-12, p. 268. Classification systems are not strictly comparable. Changes slightly overstate numbers of laborers and service workers in 1973 and understate operatives.

4. James G. Scoville, *The Job Content of the U.S. Economy, 1940-1970* (New York: McGraw-Hill, 1969).

5. Richard S. Eckaus, "Economic Criteria for Education and Training," *Review of Economics and Statistics,* May 1964. For a more complex treatment of the data coming from the Employment Service's *Dictionary of Occupational Titles,* see Ivar Berg's *Education and Jobs, The Great Training Robbery* (New York: Praeger, 1970).

6. William V. Deutermann, "Educational Attainment of Workers, March 1973," *Monthly Labor Review,* January 1974, p. 58. Deutermann has used the arithmetic mean rather than the familiar median years of school completed, "(b)ecause the major changes occurring in the educational attainment of the population and labor force have been concentrated at the extremes of the educational distribution, (and) the arithmetic mean is a more sensitive measure of these changes than is the median. The median is particularly insensitive to these changes because over one-third of the labor force is concentrated within the median interval of 12 years. Under these circumstances, it is felt that the mean, rather than the median, is a more useful measure of changes in the central tendency of the educational distribution of workers by years of schooling."

7. Harold L. Sheppard and Neal Q. Herrick, *Where Have All the Robots Gone?* Prepared under the auspices of the Upjohn Institute for Employment Research (New York: The Free Press, 1972).

8. For a recent account of what happened—and what it meant—see James O'Toole, "Lordstown: Three Years Later," *Business and Society Review,* Spring 1975

9. Robert L. Kahn, "The Meaning of Work: Interpretation and Proposals for Measurement," in *The Human Meaning of Social Change,* ed. Angus Campbell and Phillip E. Converse (New York: Russell Sage Foundation, 1972), pp. 173-174.

10. R. P. Quinn, *et. al.,* "Evaluating Working Conditions in America," *Monthly Labor Review,* November 1973, p. 32.

11. *Job Satisfaction: Is There a Trend?* (U.S. Department of Labor, Manpower Research Monograph No. 30, 1974), p. 6.

12. *Changing Youth Values in the 70's* (Daniel Yankelovich, Inc., 1974), p. 24.

13. Harold Wool, "What's Wrong with Work in America?—A Review Essay," *Monthly Labor Review,* March 1973, and Peter Henle, "Economic Effects: Reviewing the Evidence," in *The Worker and The Job: Coping with Change,* ed. Jerome M. Rosow, The American Assembly, Columbia

University (Englewood Cliffs, N.J.: Prentice-Hall, Inc., 1974).

14. Harold L. Sheppard and Neal Q. Herrick, op. cit., p. 193.

15. Daniel Yankelovich, "The Meaning of Work," in Jerome M. Rosow, ed., *op. cit.*

16. *Work in America:* Report of a Special Task Force to the Secretary of Health, Education, and Welfare, prepared under the Auspices of the W.E. Upjohn Institute for Employment Research (Cambridge, Mass.: The MIT Press, 1973). The Task Force wa chaired by James O'Toole. For more detail, see the recent book *Work and the Quality of Life, Resource Papers for Work in America,* edited by James O'Toole.

## CHAPTER 6

1. Imogene E. Oakes, *Adult Education Participants and Participation, 1972, Full Report* (to be published by the National Center for Educational Statistics).

2. Carnegie Commission on Higher Education, *Toward A Learning Society,* "Alternative Channels to Life, Work and Service" (New York: McGraw-Hill, 1973).

3. All of the following data are taken from Imogene E. Oakes, *op. cit.,* unless otherwise cited.

4. U.S. Civil Service Commission, *Employee Training in Federal Service, FY 1971* (Washington, D.C.: U.S. Government Printing Office, 1972), p.2.

5. Special Tabulations in the *Sixth Annual Report of the National Advisory Council on Extension and Continuing Education* (1973).

6. *Major Collective Bargaining Agreements: Training and Retraining Provisions* (Bureau of Labor Statistics, Bulletin No. 1425-7, 1969), p. 8.

7. *Characteristics of Agreements Covering 1,000 Workers or More, July 1, 1972* (Bureau of Labor Statistics, Bulletin No. 1784, 1973).

8. *1975 Budget of the United States, Special Analysis* (Washington, D.C.: U.S. Government Printing Office, 1974), pp. 127-128.

9. Data from the *Sixth Annual Report of the National Advisory Council on Extension and Continuing Education* (1973).

10. Source: American Council on Education, Washington, D.C.

11. Source: Educational Testing Service, Princeton, N.J.

12. *Recurrent Education: A Strategy for Lifelong Learning* (Paris: Centre for Educational Research and Innovation [CERI] of the Organization for Economic Co-operation and Development, 1973), p. 18.

13. For full discussion of the recurrent education experience in Europe see: Herbert E. Striner, *Continuing Education as a National Capital Investment* (The W. E. Upjohn Institute for Employment Research, March 1972); Rudolph, *et al., Recurrent Education in the Federal Republic of Germany* (Paris: CERI of OECD, 1972); *Working Party on the Re-training of Adults* (1969), draft reports for OECD: *Re-training of Adults in Sweden,* 1968; *Labour and Automation-Manpower Adjustment Programmes: I-France,*

*Federal Republic of Germany, United Kingdom,* (Geneva: International Labour Office, 1967—On Britain's Industrial Training Act of 1964); *Adult Training as an Instrument of Active Manpower Policy,* Report by the Manpower and Social Affairs Committee (Paris: OECD, 1972); *Working Party on the Re-training of Adults (1969),* draft reports for OECD: *Re-training of Adults in the United Kingdom,* 1968; Carnegie Commission on Higher Education, *New Students and New Places—Policy for the Future Growth and Development of American Higher Education* (New York: McGraw-Hill, 1971), Chapter 8 on Britain's Open University.

14. Herbert E. Striner, *op. cit.,* Chapter III, "The French Venture."

15. Ewan Clague and Leon Greenberg, "Technological Change and Employment," *Monthly Labor Review,* July 1962.

16. Dominic Sorrentino, "Trade Adjustment Assistance to Workers Displaced by Imports, Fiscal 1963-73," *Monthly Labor Review,* January 1974, p. 63.

17. *Statistical Abstract of the United States 1973* (U.S. Department of Commerce, Social and Economic Statistics Administration, Bureau of the Census), Chart No. 791, "Industrial and Commercial Failures—Number and Liabilities: 1946-1972," p. 487.

18. These data were provided to the Congress by the Department of Health, Education, and Welfare, based on an updating to 1973 of findings of the 1966 *Social Security Administration Survey of the Disabled.*

19. 1970 *Census of Population,* Volume PC(2)-7E, "Occupation and Residence in 1965."

20. Harold Goldstein and William Delaney, "The Need for Job Related Training Throughout Adult Life." The National Manpower Institute, 1974. (Mimeographed.)

21. Department of Labor, Manpower Administration, *Job Changing and Manpower Training,* Manpower Report No. 10, June 1964.

22. Goldstein and Delaney, *op. cit.,* p. 16.

23. Sar A. Levitan and Robert Taggart, "Employment and Earning Inadequacy: A Measure of Worker Welfare," *Monthly Labor Review,* October 1973, p. 19.

24. William J. Grinker, Donald D. Cooke, and Arthur W. Kirsch, *A Study of Employee Advancement in Eleven Industries* (The American Foundation on Automation and Employment, January 1969).

25. *Survey of Working Conditions* (Ann Arbor: Survey Research Center, The University of Michigan, under contract with the Employment Standards Administration, U.S. Department of Labor, 1971).

## CHAPTER 7

1. Dorothee K. Vogt, *Literacy Among Youths 12-17 Years* (U.S. Department of Health, Education, and Welfare, Public Health Service, Health Resources Administration, National Center for Health Statistics;

Vital and Health Statistics—Series 11-131, December 1973).

2. Imogene E. Oakes, *op. cit.*

3. Commission on Non-Traditional Study. "Diversity by Design (an abstract of the major findings and recommendations in the Commission on Non-Traditional Study's forthcoming final report)." (Mimeographed.) The 26-member Commission, an independent group of leaders in education and related fields, is sponsored by the College Entrance Examination Board and Educational Testing Service. Their research was conducted by the Educational Testing Service.

4. Consultant's report to the National Manpower Institute by Walter LeBaron. These figures are illustrative. There are small amounts added by the federal government, and there are other special categories such as adult vocational education.

5. Alan Cartter, "The Future Financing of Postsecondary Education" (ACE Conference, October 1973). See also the Carnegie Commission on Higher Education's Report, *Higher Education: Who Pays? Who Benefits? Who Should Pay?* (New York: McGraw-Hill, 1973); Gosta Rehn, *Prospective View on Patterns of Working Time,* Report No. 1B, (Paris: OECD, 1972); Herbert E. Striner, *Continuing Education as a National Capital Investment* (The Upjohn Institute, 1971); Selma Mushkin, "Statewide Conference on Financing Postsecondary Education"(Minnesota Higher Education Coordinating Commission, November 1973). (Mimeographed); John F. Cotton, "Education Finance Reform" (The Adlai Stevenson Institute of International Affairs, 1973) (Mimeographed); Stephen P. Dresch, "U.S. Public and the Evolutionary Adaptability of Postsecondary Education." Higher Education Research Project Report No. 2 (Yale University, 1973).

6. Source: Office of Research, Legislation and Program Policies, Unemployment Insurance Service, Manpower Administration.

7. "State Unemployment Insurance Criteria for Approved Training and Education: A Survey of the States," National Manpower Institute Staff paper, 1974. (Mimeographed.)

8. *Adult Training as an Instrument of Active Manpower Policy* (Paris: OECD, 1972).

9. "Needed: A Program," *The New York Times,* January 28, 1975, Editorial section.

10. K. Patricia Cross, *Beyond the Open Door* (San Francisco: Jossey-Bass, 1971), p. 164.

11. Ann Miller, *Current Occupation and Past Training of Adult Workers,* Statistical Evaluation Report No. 7 (Office of Statistical Standards).

12. H. James Neary, "The BLS Pilot Survey of Training in Industry," *Monthly Labor Review,* February 1974, p. 26.

13. U.S. Department of Labor, Manpower Administration, *Training in Private Industry: Policies, Attitudes and Practices of Employers in Greater Cleveland* (Manpower Research Monograph No. 22, 1971).

14. Gary Becker, *Human Capital* (New York: Columbia University Press,

1964), pp. 11-29.

15. Task Force on Occupational Training in Industry, *A Government Commitment to Occupational Training in Industry, 1968.*

16. For a recent evaluation, see Maureen Woodhall, "Investment in Industrial Training: an Assessment of the Effects of the Industrial Training Act on the Volume and Costs of Training," in *British Journal of Industrial Relations,* March 1974.

17. U.S. Department of Labor, Manpower Administration, *Job Changing and Manpower Training* (Manpower Report No. 10, June 1964).

18. Peter Henle and Raymond Schmitt, "Pension Reform: The Long Hard Road to Enactment," *Monthly Labor Review,* November 1974, p. 3.

19. Benjamin Shimberg, Barbara F. Esser, and Daniel H. Kruger, *Occupational Licensing: Practices and Policies,* A Report of the Educational Testing Service (Washington, D.C.: Public Affairs Press, 1972).

20. U.S. Department of Labor, Manpower Administration, *Occupational Licensing and the Supply of Nonprofessional Manpower* (Manpower Research Monograph No. 11, 1969).

21. Beatrice G. Reubens, "Manpower Training in Japan," *Monthly Labor Review,* September 1973, pp. 21-22.

22. Calculation based on data from the Manpower Administration, Division of Employment Service Data and Cost Analysis; and the 1974 *Manpower Report of the President,* Table A-1, p. 253.

23. *New Patterns for Working Time* (International Conference Report, 1973) pp. 3-5.

24. For a sampling, see: A. O. Elbing, Herman Gadon, and John Gordon, "Flexible Working Hours: It's About Time," *Harvard Business Review,* January-February 1974; Kenneth E. Wheeler, "The Four-Day Week," *AMA Research Report* (New York: 1972); H. Allenspach, "Working Hours Per Week and Day—Flexible Working Time" (Paris; OECD, 1973); Janice Hedges, "New Patterns for Working Time," *Monthly Labor Review,* February 1973; Neil Martin, "Can the Four-Day Week Work?" Dun's Presidents' Panel, *Dun's,* July 1971.

25. Jerome M. Rosow, ed., *op. cit.,* p. ix.

## CHAPTER 8

1. Women hold 39 percent of the jobs in the national work force. "Women Workers Today" (U.S. Department of Labor, Employment Standards Administration, Women's Bureau, 1974 [revised]).

2. *Ibid.,* p. 6. In 1973 The Council of Economic Advisors estimated that "a differential, perhaps on the order of 20 percent, between the earnings of men and women remains after adjusting for factors such as education, work experience during the year, and even lifelong work experience."

3. Sources: U.S. Office Education (1971 and 1972); and National Education Association (1971).

4. "Facts About Women Heads of Households and Heads of Families" (U.S. Department of Labor, Employment Standards Administration, Women's Bureau).

5. "Why Women Work " (U.S. Department of Labor, Employment Standards Administration, Women's Bureau, March 1974).

6. *Day Care Services: Industry's Involvement* (U.S.Department of Labor, Employment Standards Administration, Women's Bureau, Bulletin 296).

7. Donald McDonald, "The Liberation of Women," *The Center Magazine*, Volume V, Number 3, May/June 1972, p. 31.

8. *Day Care Services: Industry's Involvement, op. cit.,* p. 3.

9. *Employment and Earnings,* Vol. 21. No. 7, January 1975 (Washington, D.C.: U.S. Government Printing Office), p. 142.

10. In 1971, *The Spokeswoman* predicted that in the fall there would be 104,000 new teaching graduates unable to find work against 122,000 for whom there would be positions. *The Spokeswoman,* Vol. 2, No. 3, September 1, 1971.

11. Eleanor E. Maccoby, "Sex Differences in Intellectual Functioning," in *The Development of Sex Differences,* ed. Eleanor E. Maccoby, (Palo Alto, California: Stanford University Press, 1966).

12. Matina Horner, "Toward an Understanding of Achievement-Related Conflicts in Women," *Journal of Social Issues,* 1972.

13. "WOW/Careers for Peers" (Washington, D.C.: Washington Opportunities for Women).

14. Sources: U.S. Office of Education (1971 and 1972); National Education Association (1971); American Bar Association, *Law Schools & Bar Admission Requirements, A review of legal education in the United States— Fall 1974* (Chicago: American Bar Association, Section of Legal Education and Admissions to the Bar, 1975), p. 37; and American Medical Association, Chicago, Illinois.

15. Anne M. Heiss, *Challenges to Graduate Schools* (San Francisco: Jossey-Bass, 1970), as quoted in *Opportunities for Women in Higher Education,* A Report and Recommendations by the Carnegie Commission on Higher Education (New York; McGraw-Hill, September 1973), p. 93.

16. "Better Jobs for Women," *The New Woman's Survival Catalog, op. cit.,* p. 161.

17. Labor Department figures quoted in *The New Woman's Survival Catalog, op. cit.,* p. 167.

18. Sar A Levitan, William B. Johnston, and Robert Taggart, *Still a Dream: The Changing Status of Blacks Since 1960* (Cambridge, Mass.: Harvard University Press, 1975), p. v.

19. *Employment and Earnings, op. cit.,* p. 45.

20. *Ibid.,* Table 9, p. 143, and Table 10, p. 144 (1974 data).

21. William V. Deutermann, *op. cit.,* p. 1.

22. Rates as multiples of white rate calculated from data in the 1974 *Manpower Report of the President,* Table A-5, p. 259.
The deterioration in the white/black unemployment ratio for teenagers is

dramatic enough to warrant an historical note. Since the beginning of systematic measurement of black/white differentials in youth unemployment, the ratios have been worsening. This was first brought out—using previously unpublished data—in *One Third of a Nation,* a report of the President's Task Force on Manpower Conservation, chaired by Willard Wirtz, then Secretary of Labor. The chart on page six shows the unemployment rate for white teenage males being *higher* than for their black (nonwhite, to be exact) counterparts, in the late 1940s. The rates followed closely together until the 1954 recession, when the black rate climbed sharply above the white rate—reaching roughly a two to one ratio by 1958.

23. U.S. Bureau of Labor Statistics.

24. Senate Report No. 93-147, *Developments in Aging: 1972 and January—March 1973,* A Report of the Senate Committee on Aging, U.S. Senate, May 10, 1973, p. 72.

25. A. C. Laufer and W. M. Fowler, Jr., "Work Potential of the Aging," *Industrial Gerontology,* No. 12, Winter 1972, p. 99.

26. Sidney Cobb and Stanislav V. Kasl, "Some Medical Aspects of Unemployment," *Industrial Gerontology, op. cit.,* pp. 8-15.

27. *The Older American Worker; Age Discrimination in Employment,* Report of the. Secretary of Labor to Congress under Section 715 of the Civil Rights Act of 1964, June 1965, p. 21.

28. Irvin Sobel, "Older Worker Utilization Patterns: Human Capital Approach," *Industrial Gerontology,* No. 13, Spring 1972, p. 6.

29. Virginia P. Reno, "Compulsory Retirement Among Newly Entitled Workers: Survey of New Beneficiaries," *Social Security Bulletin,* March 1972.

30. *Improving the Age Discrimination Law,* A Working Paper prepared for use by the Special Committee on Aging, United States Senate (Washington, D.C.: U.S. Government Printing Office, September 1973), p. 16.

31. H. Charles Pyron, "Preparing Employees for Retirement," *Personnel Journal,* September 1969.

32. Roger O'Meara, "Retirement, The Eighth Age of Man," *The Conference Board Record,* Vol. XI, No. 10, October 1974.

33. See *A National Policy for Older Americans,* developed by the National Council of Senior Citizens, Washington, D.C., 1975, pp. 11-28.

## CHAPTER 9

1. Alfred W. Stonier and Douglas C. Hague, *A Textbook of Economic Theory* (London: Longmans Green, 1957), p. 234.

2. See particularly Gary S. Becker, *op. cit.*

3. Lester Thurow, *Investment in Human Capital* (Belmont, Calif.: Wadsworth Publishing Co., 1970).

4. Ernst W. Stromsdorfer, *Review and Synthesis of Cost-Effectiveness*

*Studies of Vocational and Technical Education* (Columbus, Ohio: The Center for Vocational and Technical Education, Ohio State University, January 1972).

5. Most recently in Michael E. Borus and Charles Buntz, "Problems and Issues in the Evaluation of Manpower Programs," *Industrial and Labor Relations Review,* January 1972.

6. Daniel S. Hamermesh, "Potential Problems in Human Capital Theory," 26th Annual Winter Proceedings of the Industrial Relations Research Association.

7. Michael J. Piore, "The Importance of Human Capital Theory to Labor Economics," 26th Annual Winter Proceedings of the Industrial Relations Research Association.

8. Paul C. Glick and Herman P. Miller, "Educational Level and Potential Income," *American Sociological Review,* 21, 1956.

9. Dael Wolfle and Joseph G. Smith, "The Occupational Value of Education for Superior High-School Graduates," *Journal of Higher Education* 27, April 1956.

10. Herman P. Miller, "Life-time Income and Economic Growth," *American Economic Review* 55, September 1965.

11. Gary Becker, *op. cit.;* Gioria Hanoch, "Personnel Earnings and Investment in Schooling" (PhD dissertation, University of Chicago, 1965); W. Lee Hansen, "Total and Private Rates of Return on Investment in Schooling," *Journal of Political Economy,* 71, April 1963; Shane J. Hunt, "Income Determinants for the College Graduate and Return to Educational Investment," *Yale Economic Essays* 3, Fall 1963; Daniel C. Rogers, "Private Rates of Return to Education in the United States: Case Study" (PhD dissertation, Yale University, 1967).

12. Edward F. Denison, *Accounting for United States Economic Growth 1929-1969* (Washington, D.C.: The Brookings Institution, 1974), p. 132.

13. Based on Alan LeBel's research as a consultant to the National Manpower Institute.

14. Orley Ashenfelter, "Manpower Training and Earnings," *Monthly Labor Review,* April 1975, p. 48.

15. Dr. Taylor is with the Quality of Working Life Program, Graduate School of Management, University of California, Los Angeles.

16. William Nordhaus and James Tobin, "Is Growth Obsolete?"in *Economic Research: Retrospect and Prospect* (New York: National Bureau of Economic Research, 1972).

17. *Social Indicators 1973* (Washington, D.C.: U.S. Government Printing Office, 1974).

# Index

# Index